Coming Through the Fire

Coming Through the Fire: Preparing for Battle
Copyright© 2018 Calli J. Linwood

All rights reserved. No part of this publication may be reproduced, stored in a retrieval system, or transmitted in any form by any process--electronic, mechanical, photocopying, recording, or otherwise--without prior written permission of the copyright owners and Ahelia Publishing, LLC. Any scanning, uploading, and distribution of this book via the Internet or any other means without the permission of the publisher is illegal and punishable by law.

Scriptures marked NLT are taken from the HOLY BIBLE, NEW LIVING TRANSLATION (NLT): Scriptures taken from the HOLY BIBLE, NEW LIVING TRANSLATION, Copyright© 1996, 2004, 2007 by Tyndale House Foundation. Used by permission of Tyndale House Publishers, Inc., Carol Stream, Illinois 60188. All rights reserved. Used by permission.

Scriptures marked NKJV are taken from the NEW KING JAMES VERSION (NKJV): Scripture taken from the NEW KING JAMES VERSION®. Copyright© 1982 by Thomas Nelson, Inc. Used by permission. All rights reserved.

All journal entries and appendix articles are taken directly, as they were written, from the author's personal journal. All names have been changed to protect the privacy of the individuals.

ISBN# 978-1-988001-37-1

Published in the United States of America
Printed in the United States of America

www.aheliapublishing.com
aheliapublishing@outlook.com

To contact Calli directly, please email Cjlinwood@outlook.com

Coming Through the Fire

Preparing for Battle

Calli J. Linwood

Books by Calli ...

Book I : Walking Tall
Healing from domestic violence, abuse and trauma

Book II : Break Forth
Becoming victorious over a past of abuse, trauma and domestic violence

Book III : Coming Through the Fire
Preparing for Battle

Coming Soon : Call of the Warrior
Engaging in Battle

Prophetic word - August 2012

I felt the Lord was saying you are a transformed girl. The Lord wants to really commend you for the work you have allowed Him to do inside of you, because you could have blocked it. You could have run away. It took courage for you to really open yourself up and present yourself on the altar to the Lord.

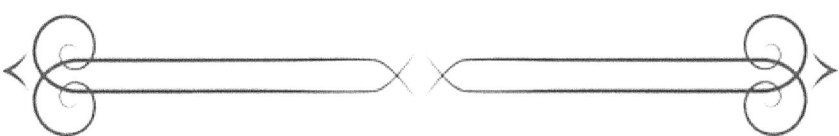

Prophetic word - January 2014

The Lord knows who are His, and everyone can see it. The enemy knows the Lord's seal of approval is upon you, His seal of ownership. The enemy has tried to steal, kill and destroy, but that seal has always remained. No one has been able to take it off. It has been so secure. God has always had His seal on you, and the enemy has hated it. That is why there has been so much attack against you—because it has been so maddening to him. But God is going to continue to walk with you every day, every day, every day.

And it shall come to pass in all the land,"
Says the LORD,
"That two-thirds in it shall be cut off and die,
But one-third shall be left in it:
I will bring the one-third through the fire,
Will refine them as silver is refined,
And test them as gold is tested.
They will call on My name,
And I will answer them.
I will say, 'This is My people';
And each one will say, 'The LORD is my God.'"
Zechariah 13:8–9 (NKJV)

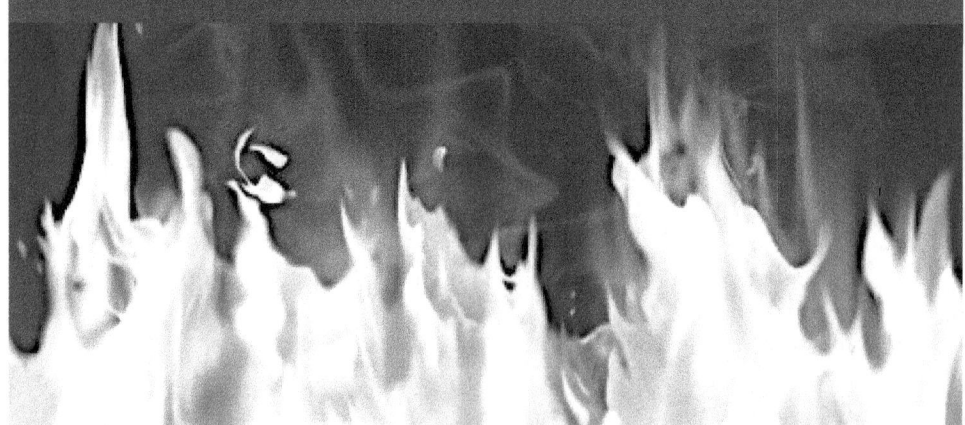

Table of Contents

Introduction	pg. 8
1–Ground Zero	pg. 13
2–In His Time	pg. 26
3–Casting Cares	pg. 34
4–Surrendering the Little Ones	pg. 42
5–Stop Trying to Figure it All Out	pg. 49
6–The Way Before Me	pg. 61
7–The Pit of Compare	pg. 68
8–Eggs in a Basket	pg. 79
9–Put Your Heart on Me	pg. 89
10–Sexual Purity	pg.101
11–Sexual Restoration	pg.114
12–Walking Through the Grief	pg.123
13–Receiving God's Love	pg.133
14–Inheritance Word	pg.141
A Final Word	pg.160
War Cry Declarations	pg.162
Endnotes	pg.170
About the Author	pg.171

Coming Through the Fire

Dear Reader,

The battle lines have been drawn and the Lord God Almighty is calling you up to fight on the front lines. But do not fear. He will never leave you unprepared. He wants to purify your heart, removing more and more of the world, and bringing it fully alive with more of Himself. As you draw closer in to the Father's heart, you are strengthened and encouraged. As you align with Him, stepping into His perfect will, you are given the authority you need to break through the barriers holding you back. And then you can also lead others through these same barriers strategically placed as blockades in their lives.

It is a mighty thing, being prepared for battle. This time of preparation is painful, yet tender and sweet. It is a time when you are being held gently in your Father's arms through the pain, as He molds, shapes and chisels you, bringing you more into His likeness. It is a time filled with violent mercy and grace, absolute surrender and stoic boldness as He captures your heart. He journeyed with me through this exact process, asking me to record everything, so I could share it here, with you. As you connect deeper with the Lord, be ready for Him to overwhelm and captivate you with the depth of His love. A new determination rises up within you as you receive your new backbone of steel and set your face as flint. Your path is set. It is time to start walking it out. Arise, my friend, my fellow warrior, and begin another stage of your journey.

I encourage you to read and pray through all the chapters, even if they do not outwardly resonate with you. At times, we do not even realize something is hindering us until part of it is unburied. Or perhaps, and just as importantly, the Lord is putting a tool in your hands for someone else; perhaps even for someone you will only meet tomorrow.

Coming Through the Fire

Though this book stands alone, it is part of a series. My first book, *Walking Tall*,[1] describes my journey of living in, leaving, and picking up the pieces from an abusive marriage, and how God set me on the right path to healing. It provides insight into the nature and dynamics of abusive relationships and exposes the reality of life in that situation. I shared my healing journey through my journals and my experiences, and I guide the reader through specific prayers to bring healing into their own lives. It is definitely more graphic than the next two books, but it was necessary in the context of telling the raw truth of my story. The second book, *Break Forth*,[2] continues to focus on emotional healing, but further expands into areas that help you take ground for God's Kingdom and live the Christian life God has designed for you. If you have had a traumatic past or know someone who has, I strongly urge you to backtrack at some point and walk through those books as well.

As you come to the end of each healing and teaching section, you will find a prayer. I did not write these prayers—I only edited them. They are Holy Spirit led and God-breathed. The Lord carefully and precisely fashioned each prayer team and time, leading us to pray in a way that reflected His heart for you. There is more power in the spoken word than you might presently understand. Pray these prayers out loud in a safe place, where you can allow the emotion and pain to flow freely if need be. It is God's heart to heal you, but healing often comes with the pain of release, and the pain of birthing something new. Allow yourself the freedom and grace to walk through the pain, so you can receive the healing that comes on its heels.

It is in the prayers that Holy Spirit power of this book is released, and you can begin to walk at the height to which God is calling you.

I give the prayer team a huge, heart-felt thank-you for coming through the fire with me in this project. It could not have been

Coming Through the Fire

accomplished without you. Your connection to Holy Spirit in your prayers will bring healing and growth to many people, growing God's army. You are truly a blessing to me and to all the readers.

The names of the parties involved, including my own, have been omitted or changed to protect privacy and honor all those involved.

♥ *Calli J. Linwood*

> "For the Lord GOD will help me;
> Therefore I will not be disgraced;
> Therefore I have set My face
> like a flint,
> And I know that I will
> not be ashamed.
> He is near who justifies me;
> Who will contend with Me?
> Let us stand together.
>
> Isaiah 50:7-8a (NKJV)

Journal entry - March 2015

The Lord has written His name on my heart. He has gone into the deep places of my heart and taken away the pain and the hurt that so deeply wounded me. He has set me free to live for Him, through Him, and in Him. I will live a life that is honoring to Him and the high calling He has given me. He has been preparing me for a very long time. I will take hold of all He is teaching me, and run with it. He has put a lot in me that has been trying to get out for a very long time. Now is the time. I have been set free! All is going to pour out, and there is going to be so much left because He restores me daily. He is my strength and refuge. I do not live out of a place of pain anymore. My heart is full and overflowing. It no longer radiates pain and heartache, but joy, love and freedom! He cares for me. He will take care of me. He is the way! He is my way. He has written His name on my heart.

Coming Through the Fire

> The only letter of recommendation we need is you yourselves. Your lives are a letter written in our hearts; everyone can read it and recognize our good work among you. Clearly, you are a letter from Christ showing the result of our ministry among you. This "letter" is not written with pen and ink, but with the Spirit of the living God. It is carved not on tablets of stone, but on human hearts.
>
> 2 Corinthians 3:2-3

Chapter I

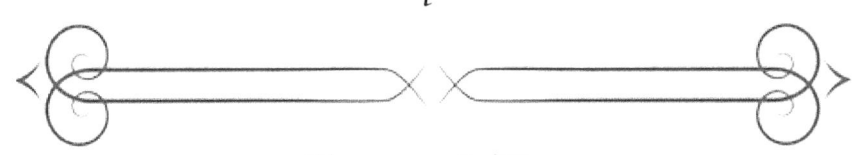

Ground Zero

WHAT!? DECLINED?? I DIDN'T EVEN HAVE TWENTY DOLLARS LEFT IN MY account? It wasn't even the middle of the month yet. I had received my paycheck less than two weeks ago. I wouldn't receive another for over two and a half weeks. There was either a problem with my account or … *How could I possibly be $600 overdrawn already?* I had only paid some of my bills and half my mortgage. There were the loan payments, insurance payments and trying to stuff a little away into savings. I had bought gas and groceries, and of course, there were the kids' school fees and extracurricular expenses, but nothing extravagant.

Reality hit me. I didn't even have twenty dollars to give my son on his birthday without going deeper into debt. *Oh Lord, less than two weeks into the month and I am broke.* I felt as if I had been slammed face first into a wall. I couldn't breathe. First I had lost my home and family life as I knew it. Then I had lost my health. And now I was wiped out financially. I had been absolutely leveled on three separate fronts. I could not take much more.

Journal Entry - March 2015

God, I can't do it anymore. Everything is crashing in on me. $600 overdrawn and it is only the 12th. Bills and mortgage still to come ... And I haven't even bought outside of groceries and gas.

I feel like it is coming crashing in on me. Do I need two jobs? Do I need to have kids quit extra curricular? Not go to camp? Not play soccer? HELP

I HAVE NOT BEEN SPENDING EXCESSIVELY BUT I AM BROKE. I QUIT. I CAN'T DO THIS ANYMORE. IT IS TOO HARD.

God, take over. What do I do?

I TRY SO HARD AND IT IS NEVER ENOUGH.

WHAT DO I DO?

SHOW ME WHAT TO DO!

Journal Entry - March 2015

Wow, Lord, that was a lot of anger, fear and self-hatred that poured out of me yesterday. It was scary when at this early time I am already out of money for the month, with bills & mortgage left, but was that coming out of me, or did I pick up on another person's stuff? I haven't felt so awful in a long time. Or was it just triggered from my own fear and shock at my bank balance and You are bringing me to ground zero financially, in order to heal it, as You did with my health, and You revealed stuff in me? If that was in me, I repent, renounce and ask for Your help and guidance. [Yes, it was my own stuff!]

  Yesterday I felt such overwhelming fear, such insecurity of how I am going to get by, such lack of trust. I could barely hold it together all day. I am so happy I am not like that always. How could Your glory shine out of me if I walked around like that all day? How could I be used in Your kingdom? I still have no idea how You are going to work this out, but it has to be Your plan. I really want to keep my house, but it is Your plan, Lord, Your will.

Show me what to do. Help me walk out of this "ground zero" in Your plan, in Your way, with Your heart and Your mind. I lay it all down at Your feet, Lord. Please guide me, show me and keep me trusting You as You walk me through yet another chapter of my story. Wow, Lord, You <u>really</u> want me to have an amazing journey and testimony at how You worked so many miracles out in my life!

I put my finances in Your hands. I lay it all down. I still will be obedient. Please remove all the fear of such loss. It is Your plan. Show me how to walk this out with grace and dignity, with my head held high! Thank You for the groceries in my freezer. Thank You for the roof over my head. I pray it can remain. But Your will in my life, Lord. Bring forth how You are going to work it out. Help me be wise. Oh Lord, let me hear Your voice in this.

Help me live above my circumstances. (Oh Lord, Your timing!) Help me to face my financial distress in good cheer. Show me Your perspective on my life as a whole.

Coming Through the Fire

Help me walk through this with joy, confidence and peace. Lead me, guide me. Show me what is important. Thank You for overcoming the world and giving me peace during my trials. Thank You for forgiving my lack of trust and angry outburst yesterday. Please heal my kids! I know You are bringing good things, beyond what I can imagine. I know I am being prepared. I have to walk through this journey, so painfully brought to ground zero in all areas, so You can build me up on Your solid foundation, into the person You need me to be, for Your Kingdom purposes. If I was healed immediately, or rescued [in my finances] immediately, I would not learn the lessons or gain the knowledge You want me to have. It hurts, but lead me anyway! Add another chapter to my story, Lord! [This was before I knew I would be writing this book series.] I pray I learn quickly!

Journal Entry - March 2015

Thank You for bestowing Your unspeakable joy on me, even in times of trouble. Thank You for cleaning house in all areas. It is like You are getting rid of everything that should not be in me: trauma, pain, anger, hatred... then issues with my health ... right to ground zero. Now ground zero with my finances. I know You will restore all of me as I am obedient. Help me to get structures put in place so I can live like You want me to live. I will trust You. Thank You for Your presence. Thank You that the more I rest in Your presence the more blessings flow into me. Thank You for transforming me from glory to glory as I spend time with You. I know You love me and are caring for me. Yes, the relationship You offer seems too good to be true, but I thank You for it. Thank You for pouring Your very life into me. Thank You for calling me to rest and receive. Thank You for the words You are speaking over me. Help me to trust You more.

Coming Through the Fire

In God's true form, He did show me—using a bush. It was not burning, but it did speak clearly! When I first moved onto my property, there were four-foot-hedges surrounding three sides of the front yard. These hedges were thick, full and healthy. Over the years, bugs and disease ate away at them, leaving the once dense leaves sparse, and many of the branches misshapen and bare. On at least one occasion, someone or something was thrown into the hedges, leaving a large gaping hole of broken twigs that could not be hidden or fixed. They were no longer a crowning glory to my yard, providing privacy and beauty, but had instead, become an eyesore, looking neglected and forlorn.

Early that spring, I made the decision to have them cut right down to the ground—ground zero. As the sun made itself known and the temperatures rose, brand new shoots grew up from the dirt. These tender young branches were coming from the roots beneath the ground—invisible but established. The branches grew sturdy, the leaves budded, and what was once barren, broken and diseased, now flourished. This new life was healthy, vibrant and beautiful. The dead was fully revived.

When I had the hedges chopped down, my rationale was that they could not look worse than they already did. I had not held high expectations for their full recovery. But as I gazed at the lushness of their appearance, realization struck. Sometimes things cannot be restored unless they are completely wiped out and rebuilt from the ground up—ground zero.

God was doing the same reconstruction in many areas of my life. And when the cutting down is in such delicate areas as relationship, health, family or finances—it can be excruciatingly painful! We feel every cut with the chainsaw, every nick of the knife as it saws away the

Coming Through the Fire

deadwood piling up in our lives. To say it is a hard process can be a gross understatement. It leaves you feeling broken and raw, vulnerable and bleeding. Sometimes you can't see past the tools of destruction, and you just want out! That would be easier—in the short term. But that is where the Lord wants us to have an eternal perspective. We are not in it for the short term, and sometimes a total reset is absolutely crucial.

After another year of seeing my life dismantled in various tender areas, I started asking the Lord when I was going to start seeing the regrowth and restoration. I could see none of the visible changes for which my heart so desperately ached. That was when the Lord took my understanding to a deeper level. He asked me to let go of my expectations. I needed to let go of how I believed things should work and how I thought they should fall into place. The Lord assured me He had things under control in the way He designed them to be; in exactly the way He had them laid out. My role was to keep walking strong in faith and in trust in Him instead of seeking things on my own. He reminded me to also let go of my own understanding. Operating within the realms of my own knowledge and perceptions only put limitations on what God wanted to actually accomplish in my life.

It dawned on me how different my perspective was from that of the Father. It was as if we were both wanting to build a house; I wanted to see the structure formed quickly or I falsely believed nothing was happening. God, on the other hand, started by building a rock-solid foundation under the ground. You couldn't see it, but it was essential to support all that came next. This way, things would continue to stand without crumbling when adversity came. If things grow too quickly, without a firm foundation, they cannot be sustained. I wanted to start at ground zero and build things from the bottom up. God wanted to start at ground zero and build things down—right into the bedrock. It takes a lot

Coming Through the Fire

longer to see visible changes when you build from the ground down. But it is then that these changes will be rock solid and everlasting. I was building a house of cards. God was building Fort Knox. Come, pray with us, and let the building begin.

Dear Lord,

    If I was lying on a hospital gurney awaiting surgery, I would have to trust the doctors. I would have to believe in their expertise. How much more should I be willing to trust You, the Master Physician, Creator of the universe, with reconstructing and building my life as You have designed?

    Father, I repent of any pride or arrogance in my words and actions that state I know how things should look and be and come about in my life better than You. Change my heart. Help me be humble in this, and completely trust in You. Let me rest in assurance, depending fully on You for all the work that will be done.

    Lord, it is painful walking in those areas of my life that have been completely leveled—taken to ground zero. I ask You to use this time in my weakness and in my affliction to strengthen me so I can stand tall and walk strong. I ask You to remove any self-pity from my heart so I can learn the lessons You want me to learn. In doing so, You can raise me to the new heights You want to take me to in this rebuilding process. Create the firm foundation You seek to instill under me, so it can support the high calling You have for me. Teach me, train me, for my heart is open.

    I pray You change my perspective on how I see these things in my life, Lord. Help me understand that You use this pruning process, this removing of the dead wood not to harm me, but to create the total design for my life that You had planned from the start. Plant the revelation deep in my heart that this process allows You to make me a new creation rather than just fixing, patching and repairing the old me!

 Thank You, Lord, for the honor and privilege it is that You care about me so much that You would start this new creation of me from the ground down. Thank You for setting deep the foundation on which to build the structure of my life, so You can transform me into all You intend for me to be.

 Lord, when one area of our lives seemingly goes so wrong, it wears on us and begins to affect other areas as well. Help me to reprioritize and refocus so I can accomplish what You would have me do. Please grant me the strength and energy for this. Help me to walk away from everything not in Your plan for me. With a restructured life comes change. Help me be willing to make permanent changes in the areas You show me so I can walk in the new design of my life in a way that is pleasing to You.

 I repent of any negativity in my thoughts and attitudes as I am faced with these trying situations. Lord, help me instead to die to myself so I can be reborn in the spirit. Help me to not strive in this remaking process, but be as clay under the Potter's hand. Grant me the trusting faith, the listening faith that will help me wait on You, lean into You, and yield to You completely. Help my attitude be one of optimism, hope, expectancy and excitement. I thank You, Lord, for all You have done, are doing, and will do in my life as You restore me from ground zero. I pray this in the mighty name of Jesus Christ.

"Anyone who listens to my teaching and follows it is wise, like a person who builds a house on solid rock. Though the rain comes in torrents and the floodwaters rise and the winds beat against that house, it won't collapse

because it is built on bedrock.

Matthew 7:24-25

I pray that from his glorious, unlimited resources he will empower you with inner strength
through his Spirit.
Ephesians 3:16

We now have this light shining in our hearts, but we ourselves are like fragile clay jars containing this great treasure. This makes it clear that our great power is from God, not from ourselves.
For our present troubles are small and won't last very long. Yet they produce for us a glory that vastly outweighs them and will last forever!
2 Corinthians 4:7, 17

Coming Through the Fire

Text from a friend, January 2016

> That is who you are and your house, your children will not fall either. They are built on that too from your faithfulness, obedience, hunger for Jesus and His truth and healing and power!

Dear Child,

I am filling you with My peace and assurance. I will walk through this with you. You will have all you need. It might hurt a little, but remember, I am here with you. I will supply all your needs. Meditate on Me. Let Me fill you. Rest in Me. Stay with Me. Your trust still wavers with each new challenge. Be a strong tree. Plant your roots deep in Me. Let your roots go down deep into My strength. I am the source. Quit relying on yourself. I will bring all you need. Put away your anxiety. Let your trust deepen in Me.

♥ Jesus

Coming Through the Fire

Dear Child,

    Be at peace. I will not leave you. You are on the right road. I will still guide you and lead you. You will not falter. Be at rest. Be still. Wait patiently, expectantly. I will show you. Keep sharing your journey. It will build the faith of others. I will bless it. I will build my Kingdom. Let it all go. Breathe deeply. I am still here with you. I am asking you to be still. Trust. Deeply. Learn to walk in peace, no matter the circumstances. The storehouses of the heavens are mine.

♥ Jesus

Chapter 2

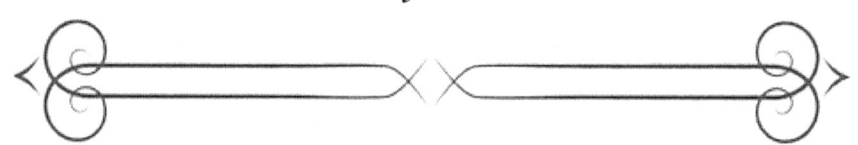

In His Time

"LORD, DO I HAVE TO BUY *BOTH* BAGS OF NUTS? THEY ARE EXPENSIVE."

"I want you to be extravagant."

My shoulders slumped in submission. "Okay, Lord."

I was shopping at one of the many stores I would have to visit that day. God had put it on my heart to buy groceries for a girl to help her switch over to an extremely disciplined way of eating so she could heal from her health issues. I had recently been challenged with this same prescriptive eating (see "Just Another Chapter" in *Break Forth*[2]) and had been almost overwhelmed by the steep learning curve I had faced. And she had three little kids, making this transition even more difficult.

Though I had felt the pressure that day from all my other undone tasks crying out for attention, this one pressed in on me even harder. I tried to bargain with the Lord. "How about if I did it tomorrow, right after church?" But it was to no avail. I felt an urgency in my heart and had run out the door immediately to complete my task. After the last item was picked up at the fifth store and several hundred dollars had effectively been removed from my already deleted account, I headed home, satisfied I had been sufficiently *"extravagant,"* as requested by the Lord.

Coming Through the Fire

The next morning, with the boxes of food now waiting patiently by the door to be delivered that night, I headed to church. As I settled into my seat to listen to the message, I almost fell out of my chair when the sermon title became apparent: "Extravagant Generosity!!" The pastor began to explain in detail about how it was not really about the one receiving the gift at all. Rather, it was more about what it did in the giver's heart.

I am sure I glowed triumphantly as I thought about those boxes in my front hall. I felt like I had passed a monumental test. It also dawned on me that had I not heeded the urgency I felt in my spirit, but instead waited until that afternoon (*after* the message on extravagant generosity), I would have always questioned whether I was more benevolent in the task out of obedience to the Lord, or simply because my pastor told me to give generously. As well, having the Lord tell me to be *extravagant* with my purchases would not have had the same astounding impact if it had come *after* listening to an entire message on it!

God's timing is perfect. It is significant, not coincidental, and always supreme. As we come to walk closer with God in obedience to Holy Spirit, we can see more and more of the Lord's intricate timing at work. This timing is so precise that it is entirely beyond human capacity to understand, let alone construct. Sometimes we doubt God's timing because it may seem what is deemed by us as *at the last minute*, or *too late*. For those of us who like to have everything figured out, accounted for and put in place long before it is required, trusting in God's perfect timing, which usually tends not to work that way, it is a bit of a stretch. But it is in this very stretching that our faith grows deep. And deep faith opens deep wells.

Coming Through the Fire

It is the fear and anxiety produced as we wait somewhat impatiently for God's answer to our prayer that makes us uncomfortable. We can also be affected by disappointment, or feelings of betrayal that well up in us as God's answer doesn't come when we feel it should come or how we feel it should come. But if we look at this honestly, much of what we may feel stems from a lack of trust that God hears us and will take care of us in the way that is best for us. And the way that is best for us may not always be the way we think it should go, nor when we think it should happen. In fact, I find this usually to be the case! I am pretty sure Daniel would have preferred God to act *before* he was cast into the lion's den (Daniel 6).

But more times than not, as we look back at a situation after it is fully resolved, we begin to catch a glimpse of the event as a whole. We start to understand the timing, and can then see why it had to happen as it did; why the timing was so crucial. So much of our desire for God to rescue us from a situation prematurely in the timing of His plans would actually cripple the development of that deep faith God wants for us. And in those situations where we still have not had this revelation, maybe we are still waiting for unforeseen things to unfold.

As a single parent, I find that many of my challenges come in the area of finance. I often battle with the fear of not having enough. But this in its concentrated form is a lack of trust in God's Word that says He will provide. Period. No excuses. I remember at one point being frustrated as an expensive item of purchase that I believed should have been split with another, all fell back on me. I felt unjustly taken advantage of and victimized once again ... and God was letting it happen. My fear of not having enough to provide for my children, again became apparent, as did my lack of trust in God's provision.

Coming Through the Fire

But the very next week, the envelope carrying the anonymous gift proclaimed the truth loudly, as God whispered to my soul, "I have you covered. Do not fear, My little one. I see you. I hold you in My hand." The envelope carried within it the exact amount of money I felt had been unjustly stolen from me. God knows. God sees. And His timing is perfect.

As we learn to be led by Holy Spirit, we develop an ever-increasing awareness of His perfect timing. That same urgency I felt with buying the groceries that day again filled my chest as I scrambled to mark a specific name on an envelope near the end of church service one Sunday and jam it into my back pocket. I had previously stuffed it with many crisp twenty dollar bills. I deliberately withdrew the money on the way to church. It could not wait. Understanding dawned as up at the altar immediately following service, I was able to hand the very person the envelope, while the words of "God will bring you provision" were spoken over her by another. Her name on that very provision spoke deeply, ensuring her that this moment was in no way random, but intimately crafted.

Again, some time later, when the exact amount of money in the card and the exact day of its delivery brought a flood of tears from the one receiving it confirmed I was walking in God's perfect timing and that He had beautifully met her needs. [It is an amazing state of heart to be in when giving away money for God's purposes is just as exciting as receiving it!]

Walking in Kairos timing, God's timing, is like hitting all the traffic lights the moment they turn green—no loss of momentum, no slowing down, no hesitation, just perfect timing. It is like hitting a fast food drive-thru when there are only one or two cars in line. But, when that person with the impossibly high-piled grocery cart steps into the

Coming Through the Fire

check-out line a half-second before you do, or when that car driving ten miles below the posted limit speeds up to make the light, and you, running late, get trapped at the red light—that too, can be God's perfect timing!

So come and pray with us. It is the perfect time to do so!

Dear Lord,

You have created the wonders of the earth with Your hand, and yet that same hand reaches down and carves out an intricate path for me, just me, to follow. O Lord, I want to walk in Your paths, in Your ways, in Your time. The storyline You create in my life is incomprehensible—the timing inconceivable! Increase my sensitivity of the impressions You put on my heart, of Your hand guiding me, in its perfect timing. Increase my sense of expectancy that You will design these opportunities where I can partner with You to create incredible outcomes. Build my faith deeper and deeper with every interaction.

I repent for all the times I have resisted Your guidance, made excuses, or didn't believe that You could make yourself be heard. Restore the blessings to the ones You called me to bless, but where I fell short. Please forgive me. Help me run toward every opportunity You present to me, with a joyful heart and a giving spirit. Teach me how to work in Your timing—outside the logic and organization of my own mind. Help me to let go of the anxiety and frustration I create by trying to force or keep *my* timing within *Your* ways. I give You my agenda. Help me be ready in all situations, at a moment's notice. Stir up excitement instead of dread with everything You put on my heart to do or say, and in the timing You require; especially when it doesn't look how I expect it to look. I release those expectations to You and wait only in expectancy of Your good plans.

Coming Through the Fire

In Jesus' name, I break off all assignments brought against me by the enemy that attempt to keep me out of sync with God's perfect timing. I remove all enemy roadblocks that are disrupting God's timing in my life and in the lives of those with whom I am to interact. Reveal to me if there is anything in my mind or heart that is also preventing me from this perfect synchronization with the Father's heart in all things. Uproot any lies I am believing about God's faithful timing, or words spoken over me, by me, or by my ancestors that are hindering me. I break off any rejection, anger, disappointment and discouragement I have received when the timing has seemed out of sync. Restore my timing so I am always walking in step with Your Spirit, and change my perspective when it is only that which makes me believe I am out of step.

Thank You for the grace with which You equip me to do exactly what You ask me to do, and accomplish it exactly when You tell me to do it. Thank You for the motivation, energy, health and strength You provide for me to be able to walk in Your Kairos timing. I do ask for You to grant me great patience to walk in Your timing, especially when I feel like I am in a season of unanswered prayer.

Help me to be aware of the needs of others You highlight to me, and be willing to put their needs ahead of my own, when You ask me to do so. Help me to see how much You are in control of my life in all the little things, so I can readily trust You are also in control of the big things, even when I can't see it or don't understand it.

Bless me with divine timing and appointments in every aspect of my walk. Let me stand back in awe and tell of the amazing timing of God I see evident in every day of my life. I pray this in the name of Jesus. Amen.

Coming Through the Fire

For my words will certainly be fulfilled at the proper time.
Luke 1:20b

But you must not forget this one thing, dear friends: A day is like a thousand years to the Lord, and a thousand years is like a day.
2 Peter 3:8

He replied, "The Father alone has the authority to set those dates and times, and they are not for you to know.
Act 1:7

But when the right time came, God sent his Son, born of a woman, subject to the law.
Galatians 4:4

Yet God has made everything beautiful for its own time. He has planted eternity in the human heart, but even so, people cannot see the whole scope of God's work from beginning to end.
Ecclesiastes 3:11

Coming Through the Fire

Dear Child,

My timing is perfect. It is My plan that we are in. Trust. Have faith. I am still building your trust and faith. All the things I have been putting into place will unfold in My time, in My way. You do not have to do anything, just be obedient and follow My leading. People need you to tell them what is in My heart for them. You will help them. My sheep know My voice; hear My voice.

♥ Jesus

Chapter 3

Casting Cares

THE UNRELENTING PAIN IN THE DEPTHS OF MY BELLY CAUGHT ME BY surprise that evening. I was somewhat used to it by now, but only in the context of receiving prayer as I sought healing for the deeply rooted trauma I still carried. Never before had this heaving, contracting pain emerged as I prayed for another. But it did not go unnoticed by Darlene, as together we prayed for the tormented one. She watched me intently and had me indicate when it was released.

Afterward, Darlene told me I was burden bearing. And so began my quest to find out exactly what that meant. One of the first things I learned was it can wreck you if you do not understand this gifting. As I sought God for wisdom and revelation, a brief picture flashed in my mind. In it, I was crying at the foot of the cross and then dancing. At the time, I did not fully understand the relevance of this.

As I continued to pray that morning, the Lord laid it on my heart that He would take care of everything—everything, that is, that I gave over to His care. So all to Him, I gave. Emotions rose and tears fell as I poured out my heart to Him in my journal, laying down at His feet everything that surfaced in my thoughts. Physical needs, material possessions, my hopes, desires and dreams, so many loved ones, my sorrow, my weariness—all were consciously placed at the foot of the cross.

With my emotions still raw, the Lord revealed that the pervasive sadness I had been feeling these last few days was a burden I was bearing for my son. I was feeling his sadness, and I needed to also give that to Him to carry. Handing it over to Jesus, I again pleaded He would show me how to bear another's burdens in a way that was pleasing to Him, in the center of His will, and would leave me in one piece with a sound mind. I still reel in amazement at what happened next. The Lord began to pour out His love so lavishly on me that I began to weep. I wept from a place so deep within the core of my being that is seemed to be pulled out right from the pit of my belly and I began to heave uncontrollably. I immediately recognized that feeling in my stomach. It was the same sensation as when God first revealed to me I was burden bearing for another.

The shock of this revelation brought an abrupt stop to my tears and to the emotion. And so began this dialogue in my journal between the Lord and I as He taught me what I so desperately needed to know.

Journal Entry - March 2015

There, I have shown you, Calli. Those stomach pains are deep, deep wounds of anguish. It is their anguish you are feeling when that happens. You are feeling their deep, deep anguish.

What do I do with it when I feel it, Lord?

Do as you are doing. Pray until it releases. That is their pain being set free. Layer upon layer I will remove their pain.

Why do I need to do it, Lord? What does it do for them? And how do I not keep carrying the sadness and pain after, so I can live in Your peace and joy?

You take the pain. I hold it in My hands. I will set them free from it through you. You will feel it for them—the deep things, so deep they do not want to walk through it on their own. You will walk with them through it. And I will hold both of you in My hands to help you through it. It makes it easier when someone is there to shoulder the load with them. It does not tear them apart, as it would if they were by themselves.

Coming Through the Fire

Why me, Lord?

Because you know what it feels like. You know how to walk through it with Me. You have been there too. But you have to make sure you keep giving it to Me each time, so I can release it from you. You will not have to carry it. That is My job. You just have to walk through with them, then release it into My hands. Give it back to Me, for it is Mine. I already carried it. Take it to the foot of My cross. That is what you were doing in the dirt at the cross—burying the pain of others, at the foot of My cross.

[The previous summer the Lord had given my friend a vision of me digging in the dirt at the foot of Jesus' cross. At the time, we both believed I was gardening, as that is something I do—although we did not quite understand why I would be wearing a beautiful, white robe while doing so!]

And up from their pain will come flowers! And then you dance ... a dance of freedom for them and for you.

Coming Through the Fire

In that dialogue, the Lord showed me how I was to bear another's burden. It confirmed the picture the Lord had given me earlier. Now I understood. It is always amazing to me how the Lord gives you things ahead of time to prepare you for what comes next, for what new thing He is leading you to understand.

Now I often experience that same contracting pain, deep in my stomach, in different situations when the Lord has called me to bear another's burdens. At times I feel it so strongly it almost throws me to the ground. Sometimes it is for a specific person, group of people or situation. Other times I believe I feel the Father's anguish for His people. Once in a while, I understand it to be birthing something for me or others. Sometimes I know exactly what it is representing; other times it remains a mystery. I simply pray hard in the Spirit until it releases.

It can also manifest as a physical pain you normally do not experience. At one point I had an unfamiliar pain in my back. Looking around, I saw a pregnant lady rubbing her back several aisles over. I prayed for her, and my pain released. It did not return.

Other times, an unexplainable fear overwhelms me, or I'll walk into a room and feel a sheet of sadness wrap around my heart. If it comes out of nowhere, I immediately recognize that I am again bearing another's burdens, and I can take it right to Jesus. Other times, the feeling has slowly and silently crept into my soul, unrecognizably tangled around my own struggles. This keeps it hidden for a time, making it exceedingly difficult to unravel this burden from those of my own. And this is where it can still get the best of me at times. Shrouded in confusion, I am not always sure how to sort out the intricate details of what belongs where, nor how I proceed to extract this burden from my

Coming Through the Fire

heart. This type of burden bearing has a bigger impact on my spiritual well-being.

But eventually, through wise counsel, prayer, His Word, and time on my knees with the Father, He reveals to me what belongs where, and then He will lift it from me as I do what needs to be done. In the end, I know I have been challenged, stretched and strengthened, thus becoming a little more efficient as I continue to be about My Father's business. And hopefully, someone, somewhere, is also resting a little easier.

Many people are carrying the burdens of another, and don't even realize it; they just recognize something is wrong—they feel different or have even been so tormented by issues in the world and that of those walking around them that they have unconsciously shut down this spiritual connection. It is not an easy task, that of bearing another's burdens, but it is so needed. Is your heart willing to accept this honor if the Lord so calls you? Come pray with me, so Holy Spirit can begin your training!

Oh Lord,

Let me praise You with all I am! Thank You for carrying my sins to the cross. Thank You for carrying all my burdens, all my worries, all my cares. And thank You for the honor you bestow on me that allows me to carry the burdens of others who cannot yet carry them on their own, to You.

I ask You, Holy Spirit, to teach me all I need to know about burden bearing so I can walk in it in spiritual, emotional, mental and physical soundness. I ask for wisdom, revelation, understanding and strength so I can walk in this gifting according to Your will and direction.

Coming Through the Fire

Teach me how I receive each burden and surrender them to You, however that will manifest in me. I realize everyone is different, and You work in unique ways in each individual. Show me how this whole process will unfold in my journey.

Please, Lord, develop an acute awareness in me for each moment I am burden bearing, so I can bring it to You as You instruct me, and not unknowingly carry it as my own, or for longer than You would have me do so.

Lord God, right now I cast all my cares, and release all my burdens onto You, for You care for me. I thank You for the privilege of being able to partner with You in this task. I pray this all in the precious name of Jesus Christ. Amen.

I am glad when I suffer for you in my body, for I am participating in the sufferings of Christ that continue for his body, the church.
Colossians 1:24

Share each other's burdens, and in this way obey the law of Christ.
Galatians 6:2

Yet it was our weaknesses he carried; it was our sorrows that weighed him down.
Isaiah 53:4a

Coming Through the Fire

Then, besides all this, I have the daily burden of my concern for all the churches. Who is weak without my feeling that weakness? Who is led astray, and I do not burn with anger?
2 Corinthians 11:28-29

Be happy with those who are happy, and weep with those who weep.
Romans 12:15

If one part suffers, all the parts suffer with it, and if one part is honored, all the parts are glad.
1 Corinthians 12:26

Then the Lord said to Moses, "Gather before me seventy men who are recognized as elders and leaders of Israel. Bring them to the Tabernacle to stand there with you. I will come down and talk to you there. I will take some of the Spirit that is upon you, and I will put the Spirit upon them also. They will bear the burden of the people along with you, so you will not have to carry it alone.
Numbers 11:16-17

Chapter 4

Surrendering the Little Ones

As I sat on the floor in the dark with the worship music filling every space around me, my mouth continually whispered to the Almighty One on behalf of my friend in need. I tried to encompass every possible detail in prayer for the plight that rocked her world. I was overwhelmed by the magnitude of the situation, and feeling inadequate. I wondered how she would be sustained through it all.

Eventually, I felt I did all I could, but as she faced the complete destruction of her family, it just didn't seem enough—not nearly enough. There was nothing else I could do. But I knew One who could do more—One who could do enough. After all my interceding, I had to now surrender her to the Lord. Only He could change hearts and lives and mend the damage that had been done.

Words alone did not seem sufficient. I needed to step out in faith with a prophetic act. In my mind, I saw my friend as she was, little and vulnerable, in a situation so much bigger than herself. I saw her as three inches high, able to fit in my upturned hands. Tears welled and fell as I slowly, tenderly offered her up to the Lord, asking Him to take her, hold her, heal her. She was His, her family was His, the situation—out of all our control— was His too, and I released it onto Him.

Coming Through the Fire

Since then, the Lord has asked me to put many other loved ones and even circumstances into my hands and offer them up to Him. From there, He led me to help others take their treasured ones, their little ones, put them in their hands, and surrender them to His loving care. As they hesitantly place those cherished ones into their hands, I can see on their faces the love they feel—a love that overpowers all, takes breath, stills hearts. Many have been carrying the anguish and afflictions of their loved ones for so long. They took the heartbreak as their own, fearful of not doing enough, saying enough, praying enough to bring the healing so desperately needed—fearful if they stopped—if they didn't carry it all, all would be lost.

Yet this burden is not one we can carry, nor should we carry. No matter how much we desire it, we do not have a way to put back together the hearts shattered by life, loss, tragedy. There is nothing more powerful than releasing these lost ones, these aching ones into the Lord's hands and trusting Him to bring what they need into the situation. He is All Mighty. He knows all. He sees our lives from the perspective of completion—knowing already how everything fits together, and what is necessary on our paths. He knows what turns we must take and the backtracks that will happen. He fully knows the pain carried in each heart, and exactly how it came to be. And, He alone knows how to bring restoration and how to put life back into seemingly hopeless situations.

So many of the answers to our prayers come from a source we didn't know even existed—couldn't know existed until they appeared. In holding the people in our lives tight, we are restricting them to our finite capabilities and resources. In releasing them to the Lord, we are allowing —even requesting—that the limitless resources of God are accessed and released into their lives. This is more powerful than anything we can do on our own, as we attempt to keep carrying them. Pray for them, yes.

Coming Through the Fire

Fight for them, contend for them, but then surrender them. As contrary as it is to our natural tendency of holding tight all those and everything we hold dear, letting them go becomes our ultimate prayer.

After walking through this prophetic act with so many others, the Lord turned it back to me and said, "Isn't it time you put little Calli into My hands as well?" At those soft words whispered into my soul, my chest constricted and I sat in stunned silence, with tears threatening my tight self-control. Why did the thought of that affect me so deeply? Everything around me went still and quiet, pausing as I did, to ponder this simple yet profound request of the Lord. I was the one who warred for others, who pleaded on their behalf. My own *little me* was not thought of often. She was busy being busy, running, scurrying, taking care of others, helping them carry their loads.

Revelation dawned—God wanted me to truly cherish myself as I had done for all the others in my life. He wanted me in His hands. He wanted me to be in the realm of His infinite supply being able to meet all my needs; those spoken, and those still held as captive secrets deep in my heart. Letting down my long-held guard, I took as much a deep breath my paralyzed lungs would afford me, and let *Little Calli* come into view. Though over the years I had received many layers of healing from the countless traumas that had shaped my world, there was still so much that infiltrated my body, soul and spirit. The act itself of picturing her, little Calli, delicate and fragile, was hard for me to bear, and the dam of self-control broke. Deep pain and sadness welled up from the depths of my being and spilled out.

Overtaken with emotion, in my mind I picked her up, this little girl who was me, and set her gingerly in my other hand. Consciously exhaling and enlisting all the courage I could find, I surrendered to the feelings for this little one I finally allowed myself to have, knowing that

Coming Through the Fire

was exactly how my heavenly Father felt toward me. I needed to honor that, and therefore, honor myself and take the same care of myself that He wanted for me. I finally understood in the practical sense, that yes, you are to love your neighbor, but you love them as you are to love yourself. You need to love yourself. You need to cherish yourself, just as God made you. He loves you and wants you for His own. He wants you to offer yourself up to Him so He can open up the heavens for you and help you, heal you, and fully restore you. You have been carrying your burdens and those of others for too long.

As you put yourself and your loved ones into His hands, though the burdens are still on your shoulders, He carries the full weight of them. So come now, pray with us. I believe it is time to surrender all the precious little ones, especially yourself, into the Lord's all mighty hands. Let's pray.

Father God,

I thank You for all the little ones in my life. I love them so very much, with every part of my heart. But You, Lord, understand this depth of love, for You surrendered Your own Son, so that I may live. And You know my heart. You know this very love I hold for those You have put in my life—a love that overpowers and takes the very breath from my lungs. But You love them even more than I do. And only You have the power to change hearts and lives and mend the damage that has been done to them. Only You have the knowledge and ability to give them exactly what they need.

Help me trust You enough to put them totally in Your care. You died for them so they can live. You died for me so I can live. It is only You who will give us *all* life. So, Lord, I pray for courage and wisdom

Coming Through the Fire

to bring the ones I love, the ones that need help, the weak, the hurting, to You, and release them fully into Your hands in complete surrender.

Sometimes Your solutions for people go against human logic, against the logic of the world, Lord, but as I release them to You, and You take over the situation, logic no longer has any meaning. You are able to bring each one to the exact place they need to be at the exact moment they need to be there to receive the exact things they need. Only You can do that. And as I release them, taking my control off of them, this is what I am releasing them into; and this is what I want for them—and for myself. Lift the veil from their eyes, Lord, and lift the one from my eyes as I surrender them unto You.

Lord, right now I put _____ into Your faithful hands. I lift them up to You. *(Perform the prophetic act of placing "the little ones" into your hands and lifting them up to God. Repeat with as many people, including yourself if needed, as are weighing on your heart. Be sure to follow any specific instructions or prayers of Holy Spirit as you are led with each person you release. Then continue with the prayer.)* **They are yours. I ask You to take them, hold them, heal them, as I let them go. Though I feel a loss of letting them go, releasing them into Your hands, it is not letting them go unto death, but I am giving them to life. I am giving them to love. I am giving them to freedom.**

Please fill my heart with peace, knowing that they are now in Your hands and that You will give them the love, peace, freedom, wisdom, healing and unity they need. You will meet all their needs, as You are the only one who knows them all and can meet them all. I receive Your blessings and peace as I walk in obedience to Your call to surrender them. I pray this in Jesus' name. Amen.

Coming Through the Fire

Yes, the Sovereign LORD is coming in power.
He will rule with a powerful arm.
See, he brings his reward with him as he comes.
He will feed his flock like a shepherd.
He will carry the lambs in his arms,
holding them close to his heart.
He will gently lead the mother sheep with their young.
Isaiah 40:10-11

I will bless the LORD who guides me;
even at night my heart instructs me.
I know the LORD is always with me.
I will not be shaken, for he is right beside me.
Psalm 16:7-8

I will contend with those who contend with you,
and your children I will save.
Isaiah 49:25b (NIV)

Coming Through the Fire

Dear Child,

    You are more than enough. You are so much more than you could possibly know. My blood was spilled for you, and I would do it again. I would give it all again, just for you. You are more precious than my own blood. My love for you overflows. You are worthy of everything I have given. You are My precious child. I want you to know how much I love you.

♥Jesus

Chapter 5

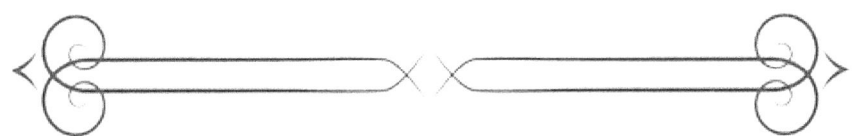

Stop Trying to Figure it Out

"I DON'T UNDERSTAND, LORD!" WE SAY.

"You don't have to," says the Lord. "I see the whole picture. I see things you do not see. I see things that will hurt you, draw you away from Me, make into idols of your heart. I see things you have no idea about, don't know are there, or even exist. So how could you possibly understand? I know your heart intimately. I know you better than you know yourself and love you with a capacity you cannot even fathom. So no … you do not understand, nor do you have to understand. You just need to draw near to Me, surrender your whole heart, trust and obey. And I will do the rest."

Coming Through the Fire

I am a reasonably intelligent, linear, analytical and somewhat logical person. I like things to make sense in my brain. I operate from to-do lists, outlines and charts. I read the manual when I attempt to assemble things, and I more often than not, read curriculum documents and program information from cover to cover. I like to figure things out and see how they fit into the bigger picture.

But this is exactly where the clash comes. We only think we know what the big picture looks like. In reality, many times we have absolutely no idea! The Lord does give us glances of what our lives will look like—our destiny, but not the full picture, with all its intricate details and dimensions. Nor are we given all the circumstances and side-trips we will discover along the route. This concept becomes clear as we look at our lives backward. How many times over the years can we say, "I didn't see that coming!" This can be in regard to problems and solutions, as well as relationship, family, career, financial and personal matters alike. Often, the situation we feel stressed about remedies itself in a manner we could never have predicted or planned. We simply cannot figure things out if they are to go the way in which God has orchestrated them. As soon as we are in the realm of God and Holy Spirit, many things do not appear to make sense through the filter of the human perspective.

Both trials and unimaginable opportunity unfold as the Lord allows, in a course of action we could not construct by our own design. He connects people, places and events with seemingly impossible "coincidences." It is like trying to find the best possible solution to a dilemma when we don't even know all the possible options available to us. God plans it and puts everything into place. All we have to do is connect the dots. We can think of it as walking out our life's journey and getting to choose between two planning committees—one that has

Coming Through the Fire

limited, finite contacts and resources, and one that knows everyone that has and will ever live, and everything that has ever and will ever happen, and has access to absolutely everything … no contest, right?!

Yet we continually make it exactly that because we feel we have to understand how things will play out, or even worse, figure everything out on our own. We presume we have to create the solutions and opportunities for our lives, and make the preparations and the plans to accomplish them. But be aware that we can end up limiting God with our plans. We limit His power by trying to keep our lives within the domain of our own understanding. He can do all things! The plans made from our human perspective do not take into account His infinite imagination and creativity, His unlimited resources, and the great miracles He can do—making the impossible possible. We can and should make plans in life. That is not wrong, but always allow God to absolutely hijack them! Yes, use the brain God gave you, but always, in everything, seek His counsel first! Do not be like Joshua and the Israelites, who were deceived into making an unwise treaty simply because they did not consult the Lord (Joshua 9). Ask the questions!

When a decision or a project is before you, always ask the Lord how to proceed. And if you do not know the questions to ask, ask Him about that too! Pray into all problems, opportunities, relationships and situations. If you have prophetic words over your life, ask Him how to start moving toward them so they will be fulfilled in His time. Though you cannot determine on your own how to *make* destiny come about, He will be faithful in directing your decisions and your steps to have you arrive exactly where you need to be. He will give you actions to take and methods to prepare. And He will open doors of opportunity to which we do not have access on our own.

Coming Through the Fire

God will also show you how to break down bewildering projects, making them manageable. When I felt I was to transcribe and type out all of my prophetic words and assemble them together, it was overwhelming to me. (I was dealing with a continual headache, aggravated by electronics. See "Just Another Chapter" in *Break Forth*.[2]) But the Lord just asked me if I could transcribe five minutes a day, and type two pages at a time. To that, I could commit, and before I knew it, the project which I had considered so colossal, was done. And it turned out not to be the onerous task I had imagined.

One of the areas in which I was intent on figuring out on my own was when I realized I was to write my story. *But Lord,* I complained, *it's too big. How does one take all the things that have happened, good and bad, and put it all together, from start to finish, so it makes sense and has the intended impact? How would I tell my story so it would be pleasing to God and draw others to Him?* As I contemplated the enormity of the task I was given, and the heaviness that would surely be its companion, I wondered, *How does one start at the beginning, when they truly did not know the beginning, nor the end? How does one know what to include, what to expose, and what to keep hidden? How does one choose the intensity of the language for the intended audience when that is an unknown as well?* It was too much. I had no idea where to start nor how to go about writing my story. At that point, I was not entirely sure what my story was, nor how such an ugly reality could be used for the glory of God. But God is faithful. He whispered to my heart, *Tell of how I healed you, for you are My story.*

However, starting at the beginning and ending at the end of my story was my plan and reasoning, not the Lord's. Instead, each day He just showed me the section I was to write. Then piece by piece, He created His design. He would show me which pieces of writing belonged together to make a whole, cohesive story. Journals, long forgotten, appeared and became a part of it. Old poems, writings and pictures, lost for years, unexpectedly appeared in an old box I suddenly had the urge to clean out … the exact day I made a reference to them or thought about them. Prophetic words spoken over me by others were brought to remembrance at the moments I needed them. (Hence the need for the binder, though I did not know that at the time!)

The order of the book and its three sections formed naturally as I progressed—far from the ordered, preplanned procedure I usually followed when working on a writing project. As I flipped through my journals, certain prophetic letters I had written in my time with Jesus seemed to be highlighted, and I typed them out in obedience. They miraculously fit with each chapter I had written, with no forethought on my part. Then the Lord gave me a plan for the prayers, bringing the people I needed, and orchestrating the perfect opportunities. And as I wrote, He brought wisdom and revelation, and unexpectedly, further healed my heart. I wrote *Walking Tall* in three months, with the prayer sections being added over the next month. It was published just four months, six days from the first day of writing … miraculous in itself, but that is another story! Writing the subsequent book became a slightly different process, as it evolved and changed as I learned how to partner with the Lord in this project, but it was none the less miraculous.

All along my journey, God has been speaking to me about not trying to figure it all out on my own. He tells me to let go of all for which I am striving. He reminds me He will guide me in His time. He has taught me that each day I grow a little stronger, a little closer to His heart, and I hear His voice a little louder. I need to stay strong in the confident hope He has placed within me. I have to stay true to the vision He has birthed in me, but understand that as I walk in close union with

Coming Through the Fire

Him, He will guide me. I don't have to figure out the path for myself. As I grasp hard onto Him, others will see my joy and feel my strength, and that will draw others unto Him. He will open doors in my life as I need them, and I just have to be obedient in walking through every door He opens for me. Though this is not as easy as it sounds, and it doesn't always seem to make sense in the natural, especially when risk is involved, it is the way God works in my life.

Above all else, I need to place my trust in the Lord. I need to believe that He has as much to do through me as I will allow, and that I can grow excited about all He has promised me. He will make me strong and prepare me for all He has called me to do. I need to do my part—reading, searching, writing, listening, praying, worshipping, being grateful, trusting, obeying—and it will all fall into place without me having to strive on my own. And to date, He has been very direct with His instructions on what I am to do in so many circumstances, and with even life-changing decisions! I do not have to worry or create my own plan for things to happen, but know He will pave the way as I am obedient and surrender every little detail to Him. He will also prepare the hearts of the other people intertwined with my destiny.

The Lord reminds me that my heart belongs to Him, and I need to keep Him as my first love, prioritized as number one, with everyone and everything else behind Him. Then He will bless me bountifully with the other things—time, matters of the heart, finances, relationships. I need to count it all joy—everything I have suffered for Him. I cannot go ahead of Him. He reminds me often of this. And I know He is there with me always. I need to believe I am not forgotten. I am loved. I am valued. I am His precious treasure and His favor is upon me. And you as well, need to believe you are not forgotten. You are loved, valued, treasured and favored. As we keep our focus on Jesus, He will partner with us in

Coming Through the Fire

His time, for His purposes, giving us our purposes in life. He is our treasure, our answer, our peace, our everything. Our lights will burn brightly as we stand with Him, and look to Him, our strength and shield. It doesn't matter how we feel. God is in control over every situation, good, bad and ugly, even when it doesn't make sense in our limited understanding. Trust. That is what we are called to do. Trust that we do not have to have it all together, or have it all figured out, nor do we have to figure it all out. Do you trust Him with His plan for your life? Let's pray and take that step of handing it over to Him.

Dear Lord,

Help me keep my eyes fixed on You, knowing You will lead and guide me, figuring it out for me! Thank You for Your direction and Your empowerment. Thank You for equipping me to go everywhere You lead me. Lord, help me seek Your will in all situations. You are in control of everything, everywhere. Help me ask all the questions I need to ask, for every situation and circumstance in my life. I repent for not trusting You in some areas of my life. Help my unbelief. Build my faith. Help me keep committed to my time with You. Thank You for showing me the path of life, the fullness of joy, and the pleasures You have for me, forevermore! Thank You for creating my heart to instruct me. Keep it soft before You, and ever-aware of those instructions. Thank You for speaking deep into my soul to guide and teach me.

Lord, thank You that my problems and situations become a perspective lifter with Your help. Open the eyes of my understanding to see more the way You see, and to know You have a better view, a bigger picture of my life than I do. Let each of my problems be a ladder enabling me to climb up and see my life from Your perspective.

Coming Through the Fire

Your thoughts are so much higher than my thoughts, Your ways are so much higher than my ways. Help me turn to You and see the Light of Your presence shining upon me. You have answers in Your hand before I even know there is a problem or I even have a question. Let me trust in this. Thank You for choosing weak ones like me to accomplish Your purposes! Thank You that my weakness opens me up to Your power. Help me live in trust and dependence on Your unlimited resources. Thank You for equipping me to fully handle any difficulties You allow. Thank You that I can relax in Your presence and trust in Your strength.

Lord, I repent for wanting things to go my way rather than seeking You in all things. I turn from trying to figure things out and questioning You. I turn from my lack of faith and doubt when things don't happen when or how I think they should. I turn away from the complaints in my heart and ask You to fill it instead with an immeasurable amount of trust and faith. I do not want to hold You back from any of the things You are doing and wanting to do in my life. I stand here now and declare that I will not limit You in any way! I give You authority over the plan of my life. Do with it as You will! I come against any spirit of pride that says "It should look like this," or "It should happen at this time." I cast down that spirit and put the cross of Christ between me and pride. I cut it off on my mother's and father's side, back to Adam and Eve. I trust You, Lord, I trust You with my life.

Lord, I may not understand, and may never understand some of the things that happen in my life, but I choose to trust You. I ask for revelation, wisdom, understanding so I can partner with You in my life more and more. I will not worry about tomorrow but daily put my life fully in Your hands, as I know You have the best possible plan and I trust You fully. I love you, Lord. Thank You.

Coming Through the Fire

Only by your power can we push back our enemies; only in your name can we trample our foes. I do not trust in my bow; I do not count on my sword to save me. You are the one who gives us victory over our enemies; you disgrace those who hate us. O God, we give glory to you all day long and constantly praise your name.

Psalm 44:5-8

Trust in the LORD with all your heart; do not depend on your own understanding.
Seek his will in all you do, and he will show you which path to take.

Proverbs 3:5-6

"Yes," says the LORD, I will do mighty miracles for you, like I did when I rescued you from slavery in Egypt." All the nations of the world will stand amazed at what the LORD will do for you. They will be embarrassed at their feeble power. They will cover their mouths in silent awe, deaf to everything around them.

Micah 7:15-16

Coming Through the Fire

For my words will certainly be fulfilled at the proper time." For the word of God will never fail. Mary responded, "I am the Lord's servant. May everything you have said about me come true." And then the angel left her.
Luke 1:20b, 37-38

Oh, how great are God's riches and wisdom and knowledge! How impossible it is for us to understand his decisions and his ways! For who can know the LORD'S thoughts? Who knows enough to give him advice?
Romans 11:33-34

We may throw the dice, but the LORD determines how they fall.
Proverbs 16:33

Show me Your ways, O LORD; Teach me Your paths. Lead me in Your truth and teach me,
For You are the God of my salvation; On You I wait all the day.
Psalm 25:4-5 (NKJV)

Coming Through the Fire

Dear Child,

Open your eyes and you will see. Open your ears and you will hear. Ground yourself in the Word. Put your trust in Me. Learn how to hear My voice clearly. I will guide you, step by step. Heed My voice. Obey My commands. Be faithful and true. Do all I ask. Let peace flood your heart above all. Rest in Me. Find your peace through Me. Let your heart be still. Keep seeking Me. I will teach you. Relax and let it all unfold. It will be a glorious unfolding. I hold the plan in My hands. I walk with you in this. You have nothing to fear. Do not let it overwhelm you with fear or unrest. Listen to My voice and guidance. I will not let you go. I will not let your foot step off the path. Obedience and desire are all I am after. Keep your heart focused on looking for Me in all you do. I will bring forth what needs to happen. I will prepare the people and the events that need to be orchestrated.

I hold everything and everyone in My hand. Your mind still wanders and tries to figure it out. Let go and let it unfold as I have it planned, not as you wish to see it. Your plans do not take into account all the great miracles I can do. Your resources are limited,

Coming Through the Fire

and they come from a human perspective. I work things out in ways you cannot even fathom, and My resources are unlimited. Keep this in mind, otherwise you will limit My amazing ways and works. Do not limit My power with your understanding. I can do all things!

♥ Jesus

Chapter 6

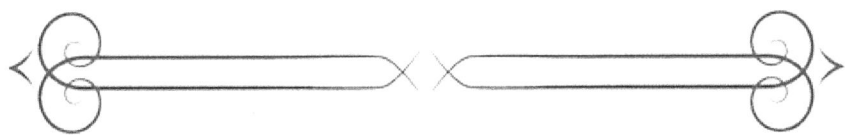

The Way Before Me

DRIVING HOME FROM MY FRIEND'S BIBLE SCHOOL GRADUATION, I unwittingly asked my mentor at that time a Bible-knowledge question. I believe it was about Daniel. Her response was unexpected: "And that is why you need to go to Bible school!" (She never did answer my question!) At that moment, I experienced my first ever deep-knowing that yes, I would go to Bible school, whether I wanted to do so or not!

It's not that I didn't want to go ... but I had been teaching for only a few years at a school I loved, with great friends in a city I had grown fond of, living in the perfect house with an easy-to-get-along-with roommate, for a director of education that had sought me out ... and all after the toil and expense of a four-year university degree. I did not want to give all that up. No way! Yet I knew, deep in my heart, that somehow, some way, I would end up there. I did.

The next time, many years later, that I once again experienced such a *knowing*, I was a disobedient. (If you read *Walking Tall*,[1] you know exactly how well that went.) Flash forward ten plus years, and it was this same knowing that put me into the Cleansing Stream[3] course where I received so much of my healing. I had heard of this program

Coming Through the Fire

several times previously over the years, but had never really paid attention to it. Somehow this time, it was different. I just *knew* I would be taking it. I didn't have to figure it out, decide or see if it would be feasible with the kids' schedule—I just *knew* I was taking it. There was no question about it in my mind. I could have fought it, been disobedient again … but I knew better!

I have come to learn this is one of the ways the Lord will direct my steps to lead and guide me on my life's journey. There really is no other way (that I can think of!) to describe it than He puts a deep, unquestionable knowing about something in the pit of my stomach. If I am asked how I know I cannot answer, other than "I just know." There is no human logic, reason, or figuring it out. It just is. What I know may be rational in conventional wisdom, or absolutely irrational … (though it will never conflict with Scripture), but I still *just know*. As I began to recognize this as guidance from Holy Spirit and see the always amazing results as I am obedient to this almost bizarre phenomenon, I began to hesitate less before eagerly jumping on board, confident it is part of the path set out for me by the Lord God Almighty.

Throughout my healing journey, I began to recognize other ways in which the Lord was directing my steps. One such way was how He directed me to go to a specific camp in the summer of 2015. It was here I received the beyond-all-doubt confirmation from Pastor Jay Pike that I was to write my story and bring the plight of domestic violence into the light. That was the birth of *Walking Tall.*[1] (See the introduction of Walking Tall for the prophetic words.) This particular camp was one where I had been a counsellor for two summers during my twenties. I had not thought of the camp since.

That spring, many, many years after the camp had become a distant memory, I saw a poster advertising it. I was immediately drawn to

Coming Through the Fire

it, wondering about its significance. A short time later, a good friend mentioned she was going to that same camp this summer. I had not heard or thought of this particular camp in twenty-five or so years. Now it had resurfaced twice in the span of a week. It was enough to evoke me to ask, "Lord, do you want me there?" He did. It was a huge step in my journey.

Around the same time, as the Lord continued to speak to me through words in my journal (see "Life Changing Words" in *Break Forth*[2]), I began to understand that He can relay directive, prophetic words directly into our hearts and they can come out of our pens and our own mouths; they did not have to necessarily be spoken over us by another, the format with which I was more familiar and confident. At that time I had not understood much about operating in the prophetic realm for myself, though I desired it, but throughout the next several months, various circumstances led me to pursue knowledge of this gifting from Holy Spirit. As my understanding grew of how to operate in the prophetic arena, it shifted many areas in my life, both in how I heard personally from the Lord, and in the depth to which I was able to minister to others. The more clearly you hear the voice of the Lord with accurate discernment, the more needless layers you can cut through to get to the core of issues both within yourself and in others, and the more clear your directional path becomes.

Another strategy the Lord uses to put steps of guidance in front of us is to put a direction in our heart or a question in our mind, and then confirm it through various people, Scriptures and circumstances. In this way, He opens the doors of opportunity and guides us directly to and through them. We do not have to invent these doors, create them, or kick them down. We just have to be obedient and go through them; (*every one* of them, *no matter* the level of risk involved, but that is for another book!)

Coming Through the Fire

Words spoken during a message at church or during a conference, teachings from books, audio and video messages, and words or pictures from friends—or even strangers—can also seem to initiate or confirm the steps the Lord is encouraging us to take, especially when the same theme is repeated. God has even been known to give the exact same prophetic words or pictures to different people at different times. This is significantly confirming, as the likelihood of that happening consistently in the natural, considering the almost endless possible combinations of pictures and words one could see, is almost nil, emphasizing the supernatural nature of this occurrence. No matter the direction He is wanting you to take, if you are listening, have a willing heart, and are willing to take the risk, He will make clear to you all the steps of your journey. You won't miss it!

Dear Heavenly Father,

All of creation responds to the command of Your strong arm. You command the heavens and they obey Your voice. The moon and the stars are under Your directive. You have guided the paths of Your people from the beginning. And now, Lord, You guide me. You guide my path and my life as I listen for Your voice, as I obey Your commands. Thank You for guiding me in Your wisdom, so far above what I could do for myself. Your plans for me are exceedingly, abundantly greater than I could ask or imagine for myself.

Open my heart and my mind to hear Your voice, and heed Your direction. Let me know Your voice more and more as I press into You. I break off any distraction that attempts to mislead me or block my ears from hearing Your voice. I shut the mouth of the enemy and leave him powerless over my life. I cut off any attempts of satan, the deceiver, to come as an angel of light to throw me off course. I bind up the lies of

Coming Through the Fire

the enemy that attempt to twist God's truth over my life and the course it is to take. I ask You, Holy Spirit, to expose these lies so I may come into alignment with You.

Lord, my life is in Your hands. Teach me to hear Your voice more every day. I thank You that You speak to me in so many ways, and You are increasing Your repertoire with me steadily as I seek You and heed Your instruction. I pray You continue to lead and guide me to higher and higher spiritual levels, so I can become a stronger warrior for the advancement of Your Kingdom. Keep my heart willing to follow You. Keep my feet on Your path. Help me be willing to take the risks in following You that You require of me. Increase my discernment that I may hear Your voice with ever more clarity, and with increasing detail. Let me hear Your voice and see Your ways in everything around me. Thank You for continuing to open doors of opportunity as I continue to progress through them. Thank You for continuing to confirm Your direction to me through Your Word, and through Your voice to others in my community.

Help me to trust that You are putting the steps of my journey in front of me; I do not have to go searching for these steps—I only have to search for You, and You place them ever so plainly at my feet; always there when I am ready to take the next step. Please develop the confidence and trust I need in You that I do not feel anxious as I wait patiently for my next step to be placed in front of me, knowing that You will be faithful to place each step where it needs to be, when it needs to be there. You are faithful, and Your plans are good. You are a good, good Father, who loves His children. I pray this in Jesus' name. Amen.

I will give them hearts that recognize me as the LORD. They will be my people, and I will be their God, for they will return to me wholeheartedly.

Jeremiah 24:7

"But this is the new covenant I will make with the people of Israel on that day," says the LORD. "I will put my instructions deep within them, and I will write them on their hearts. I will be their God, and they will be my people.

Jeremiah 31:33

"I am the good shepherd; I know my own sheep, and they know me, just as my Father knows me and I know the Father.

John 10:14-15a

My sheep listen to my voice; I know them, and they follow me.

John 10:27

Coming Through the Fire

Dear Child,

    Feel My presence as you go about your day. Look for Me in the wind, the air you breathe, the stillness of the day. My heart longs for the day all people will turn to Me and hear My voice. Pray for those around you. Pray for the sick. They will be healed. Pray for the grief-stricken. They will receive joy. Pray for the lonely. They will be comforted. You too, were once lonely. Now I am your constant companion and you no longer feel that deep loneliness. You are stronger, braver, less fearful. Your heart pleases Me. You have jumped in with both feet and now are ready to take on more. I will ask you to do things in My name, and you will do them, for My glory. You must be led by My Spirit at all times. Be sensitive to My voice. Go where I tell you. Do what I tell you. Day by day I will lead you. We will work in tandem, for My glory. People will see My glory. Be obedient. Be faithful. Be strong. Listen carefully. I see you as the warrior, as always. You will stand tall and brave for Me. I will always be with you. I will not leave or abandon you. You must trust. Hear My voice. Stand strong in your faith. See My vision for you.

♥ Jesus

Chapter 7

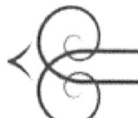

The Pit of Compare

Journal Entry - February 2015

Oh Lord, help me stop comparing myself to others! It has produced both inferiority and superiority in me and that is not what I want it to be about! Help me look only to You for my worth, my value, my affirmation. I immerse myself in Your loving presence. I am receptive to Your affirmation. Please grant me wisdom and discernment.

Journal Entry - March 2015

Lord, I ask You to choose me to reveal things of the Father and Son. I want to know Your words. I want to know Your heart. I want to know Your will. Show me how to pursue You. Show me pictures and words for others and myself that will reveal the heart of God. Thank You for what You have already shown me. Help me to stop comparing myself to others. My journey with You is mine alone; it doesn't matter about how advanced others are, or how You use them. It doesn't make me less. I want for myself whatever You have for me in my journey.

I will use you. In My time. In My way. Be patient. You are growing yet. I will give you opportunity as I see fit. You will use your voice. You will be My voice to My people. In My time. In My way. It will be magnificent. People will be touched.

I am calling you to a high purpose; yours and yours alone. Your walk is different than others. Do not try to be like them. They have their own journey, their own calling. I have a special calling for you. You will see and you will delight in Me.
Love Jesus

Journal Entry - March 2015

Focus on being you. I will direct your path; your path, not someone else's. I give you the strength you need for your path, and your path alone. Do not get confused by the journeys around you. All you need is Me. I will light your way. Each has their own journey. Each is unique, as I created each one to be. You have no need concerning yourself with the paths of others. They will have their own way. I provide each with what they need, when they need it. I am the God of miracles. Do not be intimidated. Slow down, follow Me, and I will guide you. You are on the right path.

Love Jesus

Coming Through the Fire

JEALOUSY FLARES UP IN ME AS I FEEL UNJUSTLY PASSED OVER FOR YET another opportunity. "How come I wasn't chosen for that … I would be good at it!" This is when the Lord steps in with His arresting response that changes everything: "You weren't chosen because that is not **your** path!"

So many times in my life I have felt neglected, excluded and ignored. Opportunities given to others I felt were no more qualified than I, left me feeling *less than*. Invitations extended to colleagues and acquaintances taunted me when I was not among the recipients. Facebook photos of fun-filled parties with many people I also knew … mocked me, reinforcing my false belief of being unchosen. Many times when I felt I warranted being chosen—I wasn't.

As I looked around at all the amazing things people were doing in and with their lives—all the things I wasn't doing—huge discouragement and discontentment would surge in and overtake me. Resentment would build, taking the reins of my life. I would compare my talents, my career, my family, my house, my spiritual giftings, what I was doing for God, and other such things, with that of others, known and unknown to me, and always found myself lacking. Sadness over my path in life emerged, uncovering the envy and dissatisfaction lurking beneath.

It was as if I was working on the puzzle picture of my own life, but every so often I would see a piece I liked in someone else's pile, and attempt to shove that piece into my own puzzle—and expect it to fit and make sense. It just doesn't work, and it did not make any more sense the more times I tried to make it fit. As I fell into the comparison trap, my question was often, "Lord, how come I can't/don't/haven't …"

Or, the complete opposite scenario would occur. I would rise up on my white stallion, looking down on others, wondering why they couldn't overcome their issues as I had. I would take on an attitude of

Coming Through the Fire

superiority. (Pride is ugly.) Either way, I needed to stop comparing myself to others. The outcome is always negative.

As the Lord began to challenge me in this area, He laid many truths into my heart. He showed me that it came down to the basic principle that He uses and will use each one of us in the capacity for which He has designed us. In other words, we each have a unique calling and purpose to fulfill on earth; one that no one else can fulfill in the same way we can.

In order to prepare us for that specific destination, He has put us each on a particular path, specifically designed to give us the opportunities, experiences, relationships and resources to both bring about the circumstances and to develop the character we need to walk that singular path and achieve our exclusive destiny. He uses our strengths, giftings, talents, and even our weaknesses, to forge out the perfect plan so we will be where we need to be, when we need to be there, and how we need to be. If we do not go where He wants us to go, do what He wants us to do, and become who we need to become to accomplish this, we cannot do what we were specifically created to do.

The opportunities, relationships, privileges, resources and experiences given to others are what **they need** to get them to where they are going. I am going to a different place, so as desirable as the things they receive may seem to me, and as much as I wish I could have them, they are **not on my path.** They are simply not part of my equipping for where He is sending me. They could actually interfere with the training He has for me individually.

He has shown me that I need to honor my training; honor the path He has designed for me. I had to come to a deeper understanding of what a privilege it was that the Lord of Heaven has made a special program for just me. Though it may not be easy or alluring to me at the time, this path is the one that will give me *exactly* what I need. He has carefully and lovingly devised a way to lead and guide me into becoming the very best me I can be, and absolutely able to fulfill my particular role in the body of Christ.

He also revealed to me that when I questioned Him as to why I was not given some of the opportunities I coveted; ones that others received, I was actually walking in pride and arrogance. When you think deeper about this, it shows my faulty attitude and misleading emotions. Who was I to think I knew better than the Lord Himself, as to what opportunities, or privileges, etc. should be bestowed upon me? Yes. I definitely had to repent of this on more than one occasion (still do) both in private on my knees before the Lord, and in public. (And then I had to repent of being prideful that I was able to repent of pride! Sigh—so far to go!)

Another truth the Lord exposed to me in this area was that when I wanted what other people had, I was actually dishonoring their journey. Who was I to judge whether or not that person deserved what they had received from the Lord, or to question why I too, couldn't have it? I had no idea what they went through to get where they were. I had no concept of what struggles they had to conquer, pain they had to endure, grief they had survived, or most of anything else in their life it would have taken for them to be walking where the Lord has placed them. I did not go through what they did, nor did I learn what they were forced to learn along their path, so in no way should I expect to receive what they had received, nor in any way could I carry the mantle they were now carrying, nor walk where their feet were treading.

This realization put a new respect in my soul for others' success; one that now celebrates with them and for them, rather than producing envy, criticism and judgment. This realization put such a lightness in my

Coming Through the Fire

heart that I floated right out of the comparison pit. And now, every time I feel my feet slipping down into that unstable trap, I grab hold of the Lord's hand, and begin contemplating all the amazingly good things He has blessed **me** with on **my own unique path** ... and I am grateful. He has shifted my envy to a hunger of wanting more—but the more of all that is available to me; not that of others. I intend to eagerly open and receive every gift He has available to me, becoming the best "me" I can be, for the building of His Kingdom and for His glory.

And now, my friend, know that the Lord also has a special calling *just for you.* Through all your struggles, defeats, victories, opportunities and relationships, He is preparing you for this unique destiny. He will give you the strength you need to meet all the challenges on *your* journey. Do not be distracted or confused by the path of others. Trust Him to put you on the right path for your life. You are on your own path, one unlike any other that has ever existed, or will ever exist throughout all time and eternity. Your path is *that special*! Will you honor it?

Dear Lord,

You have given me so many things; none of which are a guarantee in this life. I recognize this and am thankful for it. Help me to have a heart of gratitude for all the merciful blessings You have bestowed upon me. Let my heart be continually satiated with these abundant blessings, gifts, opportunities, experiences and relationships You have given to me in Your wisdom.

Lord, please change my perspective in any areas in which I have not been grateful, but have allowed jealousy and covetousness to sneak in. I close that door right now, and I bind up all spirits associated with an ungrateful heart.

Coming Through the Fire

Let my heart only hunger and thirst after You and Your righteousness, and every gift You have prepared in advance for me to open in my lifetime, for the advancement of Your Kingdom, and for Your glory.

I ask You to accelerate my learning so I can quickly reach all the places You have ordained for me to go, and to fulfill every assignment You give to me. I ask for a full life, the full measure and abundance in every aspect of my life that You have set out for me along my path. Keep me from comparing myself to others. Let my only measurement be how much closer I am each day to walking in the fullness of everything for which You have created me.

I bind up every distraction that tempts me into the unhealthy bondage of comparison. Help me to focus my walk as You intend it to be, in Your will for me. I repent, Lord, for any ways in which I have not trusted that You have designed a plan for my life, and that it is good. I know, Lord, that as I seek You, rather than the plan itself, You will unfold it as I learn Your ways and as I follow Your guidance. Keep me walking in righteousness, so I can receive all Your blessings. Thank You that my plan is unique; in all of creation there is none other like mine. Help me to continue to walk in this plan, while blessing and encouraging others in their walk.

In any areas where my unique giftings and abilities have not yet been revealed, I ask You to draw them out, and train me so I can use them to their maximum potential.

Coming Through the Fire

Teach me to be efficient and effective in all the paths in which You guide me. Help me to be secure in You, knowing I will be able to complete every assignment You give to me, with Your help. Please release Your army of angels in every place where I need this supernatural help.

In any places a root of bitterness has grown where I have felt shortchanged by the things You have chosen to give me, and the things I have felt You have withheld, please remove this root and replace it with an ever-deepening trust in Your design for me and in Your plan for me. Forgive me for the times I have expressed this disappointment and bitterness in a sinful and rebellious manner. For any times I have complained, criticized and blamed You, I am sorry. Please change any wrong perspectives I hold, and expose any lies I believe. Change any unhealthy and damaging thought patterns in me. Renew my mind, giving me the mind of Christ and the heart of the Father. I repent for all actions I took, believing I was justified. Heal any trauma I have exposed myself to because of these unhealthy beliefs leading to unhealthy actions and behaviors. Restore my heart to its original design, full of life, hope and joy. Teach me, Holy Spirit, how to move forward from this point in my life, and deal with this issue honestly as it continues to confront me. I pray this in the mighty name of Jesus Christ, my Savior. Amen.

Coming Through the Fire

He makes the whole body fit together perfectly. As each part does its own special work, it helps the other parts grow, so that the whole body is healthy and growing and full of love.
Ephesians 4:16

In fact, some parts of the body that seem weakest and least important are actually the most necessary.
1 Corinthians 12:22

For I know the plans I have for you," says the LORD. "They are plans for good and not for disaster, to give you a future and a hope.
Jeremiah 29:11

Taste and see that the LORD is good. Oh, the joys of those who take refuge in him! Fear the LORD, you his godly people, for those who fear him will have all they need.
Even the strong young lions sometimes go hungry, but those who trust in the LORD will lack no good thing.
Psalm 34:8-10

For the LORD God is our sun and our shield. He gives us grace and glory. The LORD will withhold no good thing from those who do what is right.
Psalm 84:11

Coming Through the Fire

Dear Child,

Have confidence in what I tell you. I can use you too, not just others! Each one is on My path for them. Do not compare ... you cannot compare. Each journey is as unique as each person. Each set of experiences they possess gives them what they need for their journey. You have the experience you need for your journey, for what I am calling you to walk. The positioning takes place as you walk in the way I have for you. You are positioned for that which I need You to be positioned. I will reveal to you in due time, all I need to reveal to you, and you will pass this revelation on to those whom I tell you to pass it. It will be okay. Do not strive. It will come in due time. Rest in trust and faith. My timing is perfect, even when you don't understand! I pull all things together with the plan I have orchestrated. It is too big for you to figure out. Have faith, strength and courage that I will lead and guide you, and give you all you need.

♥ Jesus

Chapter 8

Eggs in a Basket

> But whenever someone turns to the Lord, the veil is taken away. For the Lord is the Spirit, and wherever the Spirit of the Lord is, there is freedom. So all of us who have had that veil removed can see and reflect the glory of the Lord. And the Lord—who is the Spirit—makes us more and more like him as we are changed into his glorious image.
>
> 2 Corinthians 3:16-18

Coming Through the Fire

> **Journal Entry - April 2015**
>
> **Remove the veil, Lord! Bring freedom! I give to You, O Lord, all the idols of my heart. Do with them what You may. Reveal, heal and cleanse.**
>
> *I want your heart.*
>
> **You have my heart, Lord.**
>
> *I want your life.*
>
> **I lay down my life before you.**
>
> *Be anxious for nothing. I am here to take care of you. Put all your eggs in one basket and trust My ways. I am faithful to bring you through. Close your eyes, bend your knee, trust and hang on. There is much to do.*

DIVERSIFICATION SEEMS TO BE SOMEWHAT OF A MANTRA IN TODAY'S society. IN other words, don't invest everything in one place. Spread things around; put a little here and a little there, never give all, but always hold something back to put it somewhere else. "Diversify your portfolio to maximize your earning potential!" is the cry of the financial

Coming Through the Fire

experts. (And so you don't potentially lose all your money!) We spend time and money developing many talents, skills and abilities, and that of our children, so we will be well rounded, and ready to confront the challenges of the ever-changing world. We are to eat a well-balanced diet so our bodies receive all the nutrients they require. We need to balance work, rest and play. In the ways of the world, this strategy of diversification is logical, rational and reasonable; perhaps even wise.

But this principle does not apply in the least anywhere our heavenly Father is concerned. God is not logical, rational or reasonable in the human sense. God operates above all these things, and at a level beyond intelligence; one that is incomprehensible to us. And God definitely does not want us to diversify—hold something back to put it somewhere else—or to be balanced in any manner when it comes to our life with Him—loving Him and being loved by Him, honoring and worshipping Him, trusting in Him, obeying Him. No. He wants all our eggs in one basket. He wants us all in; totally, unequivocally devoted, with our whole heart committed to Him for all we are worth. There is no halfway in the Lord's heart for us, and He wants it the same way for us. To have one foot in the water and one on the shore is not what the Lord desires of our relationship with Him. He wants us all the way in … way in over our heads.

God desires a *David-unabashedly-leaping-and-dancing-before-the-LORD-as-the-Ark-entered-the-City-of-David*, or a *Mary-washing-Jesus'-feet-with-her-tears* type of relationship with us. For some, that means selling all their possessions and moving to where the Lord calls them. To others it means laying prostrate at the altar, heart breaking in intercession for the lost. Being absolutely sold-out for Jesus looks different for each person on the outside. It is an inside-heart phenomenon. The reserved gentleman at the back of the church with one

Coming Through the Fire

slightly upturned hand and a solitary tear trickling down his cheek may be as whole-heartedly committed as the lady with the flags at the front of the church gloriously dancing and weeping for the Lord. What may seem as overdramatic to one, is exactly what the Lord is calling another to do. (Bear in mind there are some people who profess to know the Lord and be doing His will, when, in fact, it is not His spirit to whom they are listening.)

Being absolutely committed is more so the hunger for more of His presence. It is becoming more aware of Him within every aspect of our lives, desiring to know Him more and more deeply, and expressing this in the individually unique way He is calling us to do so, as opposed to outward appearance. It is saying and doing exactly what the Lord is asking us, as an individual, to do. It is including Him in every decision. It is learning His nature at a deeper and deeper level. It is receiving more and more of His mercy, grace, love and goodness as we learn to walk with Him in more dimensions with our growing faith. It is partnering with Him for more intricate and intense assignments as we grow in trust with each other. It is knowing His will for His people as we grow in our understanding of His heart. It is not only loving Him but falling *in love* with Him. It is trusting Him with and for our very life and believing He has the absolute best for us in His plans. It is making decisions based on what He is telling us, rather than what is logical in the eyes of the world. (Please note that whatever He asks will not conflict with scripture.) It is reflecting more and more of His radiance and glory as we become more and more like Him.

In my experience, the biggest hesitation people have in committing one hundred percent to the Lord is the fear He will ask them to do the very thing they are terrified of doing, or really do not want to do, like giving away all their money, or becoming a missionary to a foreign land. But by nature, God is not like that. He is not vengeful or retaliatory. He does not specifically demand you to do things just because you do not wish to do them. True, He asks us to do things that are uncomfortable, stretching, challenging, or that yes, we simply do not want to do. But His purposes are not those of spite or to punish us. His purposes are to teach us, grow us, and define our character. It is for our own betterment, not simply to be contrary.

Another fear for a person is that they will no longer be able to do the things they absolutely love to do. But, in fact, the Lord operates so far in the opposite direction as to create a uniquely tailored destiny for us that will excite, motivate and require us to use all our giftings and talents. (He was the One to put them in us in the first place!) Walking in this perfect destiny is challenging, rewarding, and results in pure joy. The destiny He has designed for us is like wearing the perfect pair of shoes. Oh, we can wear other pairs, and trudge through life with our toes pinched, or with sore spots on our heels from being constantly rubbed the wrong way. But once we slip our feet into the perfect pair of shoes that seem like they were made for us ... the difference is achingly evident. That is what it is like to walk in the destiny God has created for us.

The true problem lies in the undiscovered attacks of the enemy as he attempts to delay and stifle the whole process of you walking in your destiny. He does not want you to do what God has planned for you, and will specifically attack you in the area of your gifting, in attempt to thwart the very plan of the Almighty. The one who is to lead worship and write songs for the nations will have lies whispered to her that instill an apathy or even hatred of worship. The one who is destined to have her voice heard by the nations to bring healing and love through music, will be told in her childhood not to sing out loud. The one who is to speak in front of crowds will have her voice stolen as she is fed lies that she has

Coming Through the Fire

nothing worthwhile to say. The one who is to go to Africa will have an intense fear of airplanes and spiders! It is the enemy's strategy to stop us before we can even start walking in all God has for us. He retains power over us only through the power we give him by believing the lies he plants deep within us. The intense fear generated by the lies fools us into believing we cannot do the very thing God has created us to do.

To keep us deceived, the enemy must prevent us from committing our all to God, and putting everything into His hands. But once we put all our eggs into one basket, fully committing our hearts and lives to God, fully trusting Him, He will bring us through the process of healing and discovery that will break the lies of the enemy. We will no longer be held captive, nor prevented from the freedom we need to walk in God's complete calling for us.

At one point in my walk I reached a threshold where everything was getting so intense, for lack of a better word, that I knew I had to make a decision. I either had to jump full in, entirely committing to everything the Lord was calling me, fully believing everything the Lord was showing me through His Word, the words of others, and the voice of Holy Spirit—or I had to walk away from it all. If everything I was learning, seeing and hearing was true, it was absolutely worthy of my total devotion. If not, I had to be done. There was no halfway. That no longer seemed to work. I made my decision. This road I have chosen to follow is definitely not easy. But this life is like no other. I have no regrets. What about you? Are you ready to jump into the deep end, way in over your head, trusting the Lord with the outcome? (Or do you at least want Him to help you be ready?) Come, pray with my amazing prayer team, so you can gather those eggs, be set free, and be made more and more like Him! (And then get on the roller coaster and hang on tight! It is a wild ride!)

Coming Through the Fire

Dear Lord,

Thank You for being *all in* when You came into the world as a baby, and when You walked the earth in poverty; rejected, beaten and bruised by those around You—for me. Lord, You struggled with having to bear the cross, taking on Yourself the entire sin and shame of the world; but for the joy set before You, You endured the cross—You were *all in* as the Lamb of God to cover my iniquity.

It is because of Your commitment to me that I could be saved and can now walk with You, in Your power and might. You chose this because of Your extreme love for me. And now I have the chance to receive and reciprocate Your extreme love by confessing with my mouth *"I am all in."* Lord God, help me to know how to fully jump into all You have for me—way in over my head, trusting You with every aspect of my being—mind, body, emotions, will, and every aspect of my life—family, friends, finances, future, destiny—every thing and every situation that lays before me. I want to make a difference on this earth, for You.

Thank You, Lord Jesus, that as You walked the earth, You were the perfect example to Your twelve apostles, investing in them, training them, loving them, and raising them up to take Your gospel of love and truth to the world—setting it ablaze as they did so. These early disciples loved You and they loved Your people; they were willing to give up everything to follow You and then proclaim You. They were hungry for You and they were committed—onto death. Lord, plant that same deep hunger and desire for You and Your ways deep into my heart. Let my passion for You burn so I can become such an example to those around me, near and far. I bind up any distractions and diversions of the enemy that keep me from Your will and Your ways for me, Lord.

Coming Through the Fire

As people look back over their lives in their sunset years, many confess regretfully that they wished they had taken more risks. It's a risk to jump in with both feet and follow You, Lord, but in the end I want to *know* I've done everything You've asked of me, and have experienced everything You've set out before me—things of You I can never be a part of if I am continually trying to protect myself or follow my own plans for my life. True abundance and fullness are only found in You.

I bind up any fear that tries to hinder this heart-commitment to You. I ask You to help me let go of all control of situations and circumstances, finances and decisions in my life, and surrender them unto You. I give You my trust. We can go as deep into this love-relationship with You as we choose. Help me to not hold back anything, Lord! Please reveal any hindrances that are preventing me from being in love with You, way over my head, so I can give them to You, and break through all barriers of resistance.

Thank You, Lord, that even though You know and have known all through history, the unfaithfulness of man, You still choose to fully invest in us—in me—because of Your lovingkindness and Your mercy. You continue to walk with us, You continue to believe in us, You continue to love us. Because of this unrelenting grace and because of Your faithfulness, we can do all things with a life laid down to You.

Help me to plant the seeds You will bless, increase and multiply to bring about a bountiful harvest that is incredibly far above what I can think, hope or imagine, as I lay down my life to You. I pray this in the powerful name of Jesus. Amen.

Coming Through the Fire

The eyes of the LORD search the whole earth in order to strengthen those whose hearts are fully committed to him.
2 Chronicles 16:9a

Let all that I am praise the LORD; with my whole heart, I will praise his holy name.
Psalm 103:1

"And Solomon, my son, learn to know the God of your ancestors intimately. Worship and serve him with your whole heart and a willing mind. For the LORD sees every heart and knows every plan and thought. If you seek him, you will find him.
1 Chronicles 28:9a

For my part, I wholeheartedly followed the LORD my God. So that day Moses solemnly promised me, 'The land of Canaan on which you were just walking will be your grant of land and that of your descendants forever, because you wholeheartedly followed the LORD my God.'
Joshua 14:8b-9

Coming Through the Fire

Dear Child,

Are you ready for more? That will come as you spend more and more time seeking Me, in My presence, learning about Me, chasing My heart. Our hearts will become more and more connected. You will have more and more peace and wisdom as you spend more and more time with me. I cannot pour My heart into yours unless it is wholly available. Lift up My name in all you do. Do not be ashamed. Proclaim what I have done for you. Proclaim what I will do for you. That is what it is about: My love for My people and My healing grace. That is what people need, what they seek, what they want. Plug into Me, be energized through time with Me. It is better than any other source of power. I am your power. I am your way, your truth, your life. I am the life all are seeking. I am the truth. I am all you need. I am all you want. Every need is met through Me. Eternal life is yours. I hold out My hand and offer it to you as you seek Me, as you trust Me, as you earnestly pursue Me with all you have … your time, resources, money, life … I am all you need. Trust. Relax. Have fun. It will be okay. You will shine, and be shiny once more. You will see.

♥ Jesus

Chapter 9

Put Your Heart on Me

Prophetic Journal Entry - July 2015

Dear Child,

    I am calling you up to be strong and courageous. Let nothing stop you. Be relentless but stay closely connected to Me. That is crucial. Hear My voice always. Seek My voice in everything. Keep connected to Me as you write, constantly checking with Me as you write. I will guard this book. <u>I will guard your heart.</u> You will get healed as you write, <u>as you expose all of your heart.</u> Depend on Me to give you strength. Be determined. Be faithful. I am calling you to much, but you are well trained. You will train others. They need to hear how you walked with Me through this.

♥ Jesus

Coming Through the Fire

> **Prophetic Journal Entry - July 2015**
>
> Dear Child,
>
> I will guide you, Little One. <u>Put your heart on Me</u>. Trust Me to lead and guide you. Think on these things: I am here with you always. I lead and guide you. I am protecting you and your children. I protect all you have given Me. You have given Me your heart, so I will protect it. Stay close to Me in this journey. I will lead you step by step. Do not get overwhelmed in the days ahead. Do not fear. I will show you the way. I am your living map.
>
> ♥ Jesus

I HAD NEVER SHARED SUCH INTIMATE WRITTEN WORDS BEFORE, BUT IF I was to have *Walking Tall* published, I would have to subject myself to having my thoughts and words unveiled. Though I had chosen one of my closest friends to first hear the words that would lay bare my soul, it was still something with which I struggled. After reading her the chapter, I

Coming Through the Fire

felt raw and exposed. I had the strangest prophetic sensation that my heart was beating about a foot outside of my chest, resting by itself on some sort of wooden object.

Later, the Lord showed me the wooden object was a cutting board. That was exactly how I felt—the knowledge that the words on the pages were soon going to be available to the public eye left me feeling like my heart, my very soul, was in a position of ultimate vulnerability, ready to be hacked up, pounded and shred. Not a pretty picture—not a comforting feeling.

Fear rose up, almost drowning me. *How could I do this? How could I let the world see every part of my pain as I walked through the torment that was my life? How could I let them see my pain, my shame, my innermost thoughts as my spirit was pierced time and time again by my lover, my foe?*

But revelation soon materialized. That was why Jesus had said to me only a few days prior, "Put your heart on Me." Those words had made no sense at the time of their writing, but I had learned to write what I heard in my spirit, and not to stray from what I believed the Lord had expressed to me, whether I understood it or not.

Meeting again with my faithful friend, we prayed. She had me put my hands on my heart, and then hold them out to Jesus in a gesture of faith. I kind of laughed as I did this, as I didn't quite know what to do with the metaphorical heart I now held in my hands. Picturing Jesus lying prone as if He was the cutting board, and then laying my heart on top of Him seemed ridiculous, even to me! But soon, in my spirit, I knew Jesus was standing right in front of me, reaching out His hands for that precious piece of me I held. Another gesture of faith was required, and with that I reached out, heart in hand, and gave it to Him. As we continued to pray, He held my heart. What a *beyond words* feeling—to

Coming Through the Fire

know the Lord is holding your very heart in His hands. There is no one I would trust more with it.

As we finished praying, I will never forget what happened next—a moment that even at the very thought of it, still has a dizzying effect on me—the Lord slipped my heart into His chest, and it began to beat in time with His. Things change as our heart beats in time with His; you begin to know the Father's heart. You begin to see His heart for His people. You begin to trust you are hearing His voice for His people ... and this stripped me bare of my fear. Knowing He has me protected—my heart protected—has given me a new boldness to step out and move into what He is calling me to do.

God has called me to be an advocate for the voiceless ones—the widow and the orphan who find themselves trapped behind a wall with no way out. He is asking me to stand strong and be their voice until they can speak for themselves. In taking my heart and putting it into His chest, He has provided me with the faith to walk in His calling for me, knowing He is leading and guiding me; knowing full well I cannot do it on my own.

I know God has a plan for my life and it is good. And I know God has a plan for your life as well. This plan will take you into the destiny He has for you. It is like Jesus wants us to build a bridge. He has designed the bridge, but we must build it. And there are so many other people waiting to get on this bridge as well. They are waiting for us to build it so they too, can use it to go where they need to go and do what they need to do. Captives are waiting to be set free. Hearts are waiting to be liberated. And their path is across this same bridge.

As you give your heart, your very life to Him, He will lead you and guide you into His plan for your life. He will show you the bridge you need to build, and how to build it. He will give you the strength, the

Coming Through the Fire

faith, the courage, the wisdom, and the resources you need to do so. He will quell the fear holding you back. He will heal the wounds that seek to sabotage all He has for you. He will hold your heart in His hands and slip it into His chest so your heart beats in time with His. Are you ready to build the bridge? He is. Let's pray.

Dear Lord,

    Thank You for the plans You have for my life. I know they are plans to prosper me and not to harm me. In them, I am given a future and a hope. Lord, I pray You give me the courage I need to take those first steps, knowing You will carry me through to the end. Develop my character into who I need to be so I can build the bridge. Thank You for the opportunities and the guidance You already have arranged for this journey. Lord, You are our map and You lead us into new territory. We can lean on You. You are our strength, and You will provide everything we need.

    I give You my fears, Lord. I give you my needs. I turn my ear to You, and I seek You with all my heart in this. Thank You for Your new mercies every day, and for pouring them out on me every morning. Thank You for Your wisdom, Lord. You are my rock and strong tower. I will trust in You with my whole heart. Thank You for providing for me out of Your glorious riches. Help me to take the steps I need to take to build the bridge You have asked me to build. I know You will never leave me. As I give You my hand, I know You build this bridge with me.

Coming Through the Fire

Help me to move forward into all You have for me. Help me put my priorities into alignment with You. I repent for allowing so many distractions to get in the way of going hard after the things You have called me to do. Prune away all the things in my life that prevent me from building the bridge You have called me to build. Give me an urgency to move forward that matches the urgency in Your own heart.

Lord, I ask for a clear vision of the bridge I am to build. I ask for a blueprint to help me build it. I ask You to open up the passion in my heart, so it may overflow onto this project. Open my eyes to the big picture. Open up the understanding in my mind, and bring revelation, desire, insight, knowledge and wisdom. I ask You to start putting resources and people to help me into place so this bridge can become a reality. Help me recognize the who and what You put in front of me to help finish this mission. Lord, allow nothing to hold me back. If there is anything holding me back, please reveal it. (Allow time for Holy Spirit time to reveal anything preventing you from moving into God's call on your life. Then ask what needs to be done to remove the barrier.)

Lord, I ask You to open up the doors to the many bridges around the world that need to be built. Lord, these bridges are needed to span the distance between You and the world, and they will also span the chasms between people, one to another. Holy Spirit, open up the visions in the hearts and minds of all the other bridge constructors that have not started construction on the bridge You have called them to build. Put into place everything they need to accomplish this task You are assigning them. Change hearts, minds and attitudes so they may make building Your bridge a priority and not waste any time.

Coming Through the Fire

Help us all be balanced in a way that is pleasing to You, but still allows us to go hard after the things You call us to do. And the harder we go after You, the more You can put in front of us. And the more You put in front of us, the harder we can go, until bridges are popping up everywhere, on time, under Your construction guidance. Help us to be disciplined, determined and steadfast.

In Jesus' name, bind up any distractions coming against us. Clear the way, Lord. Ignite the passions You have for us. Light them on fire. Put the fire in our spirits and the excitement in our steps as we move toward You. We ask for protection and for Your tender loving care as we are faithful in laying down the beams of these bridges. Thank You, Lord. I know we will build many awesome bridges together!

Prophetic word - February 2016

God covets you, He really does. He covets this time with you, the time that you spend with Him that is just one on one. That is so, so precious to Him. I just see Him holding you in these times, and just feeling your heart beat and your heartbeat is right next to His heartbeat ... He is saying "You are in sync with My heart. You are hearing right. You got this. Be brave, be bold, step out."

Journal Entry - July 2015

Talking to my pastor about Andrea yesterday, such an anger rose up, about the injustice of how these men (and women) are "allowed" to wreak havoc everywhere they go, and no one knows most of the time. They are destroying lives and families, and perpetuating the cycle over and over again, through the destructive training of their children. Lord, I know why you put my heart in Your chest. My fear, for the first time, was gone. Lord, keep my heart in Your chest. I want to be fearless. Show me how, Lord. Show me how to rise up and make changes; how to defend these women and children, the widow and the orphan.

Lord God, thank You for choosing me for this assignment. It truly is a high calling and a special purpose. Keep me in alignment with You. Keep me humble. Keep me strong. Help me be pleasing to You in this battle for the oppressed.

Coming Through the Fire

Publish his glorious deeds among the nations.
Tell everyone about the amazing things he does.
Psalm 96:3

You who love the LORD, hate evil!
He protects the lives of his godly people
and rescues them from the power of the wicked.
Light shines on the godly,
and joy on those whose hearts are right.
May all who are godly rejoice in the LORD
and praise his holy name!
Psalm 97:10-12

For God saved us and called us to live a holy life. He did this, not because we deserved it, but because that was his plan from before the beginning of time—to show us his grace through Christ Jesus.
2 Timothy 1:9

Coming Through the Fire

Dear Child,

You are on the right track, My child. I am giving you wisdom. I am still training you as you write. I am putting the pieces together, healing you, training you, stirring up the passion and anger in your heart that you will need for the battle. Trust in My design. Trust in all you see from Me. Trust in all you hear from Me. Guard your heart. I am protecting it. Our hearts beat as one. That is why it beats in My chest. I will guard it. I will protect it. I will keep it strong, synchronized with Mine. You will have more as you keep seeking Me, keep learning, keep trusting, keep growing.

Be as one crying in the wilderness. Hear My voice. Hear My cry. I am with you. I walk beside you and you do hear My voice. I ask you to do these things in My name. Not in your power but by the power of the Holy Spirit. The Spirit will be released in you more and more as you obey Me, and hear My voice. I give you the power you need to do all I ask. No more, no less. I am the power

Coming Through the Fire

you seek. I am the treasure you seek. I am yours. You are Mine. We walk together in this, side by side, hand in hand. I am your strength and your justification. You will share your walk with Me. It is for all to see My power. My glory will shine in your life. It will be radiant and draw others to Me, through you. Your light will shine. From ashes to beauty, you have risen, My warrior princess daughter.

❤ Jesus

Chapter 10

Sexual Purity

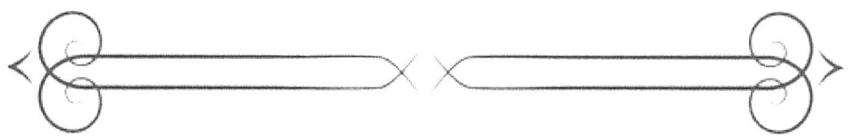

> No manna appeared on the day they first ate from the crops of the land, and it was never seen again. So from that time on the Israelites ate from the crops of Canaan.
>
> Joshua 5:12

GOD ALWAYS GIVES US WHAT WE NEED—WHETHER WE WANT IT OR NOT! Shock hit me as, driving to house church none-the-less, various sordid images were suddenly being downloaded into my mind and flashing before my eyes—absolutely random and unprovoked. Fierce horror jumped in and dread filled my soul. *Oh no, no, no, no! Lord! Not that!* It was more than just this current assault that tormented me ... for by now, I understood God had mandated me to write and share my story ... and I

Coming Through the Fire

undoubtedly knew that this too, would eventually be a part of it. I would be asked once again to put on a cloak of humility and expose all of my ugliness, so the Lord could bring healing to others. *Not my will but Yours, Lord.*

I immediately went to my house church leader and received prayer to wash and cleanse me from the images and their impact. It wouldn't be the first time nor the last I would receive prayer for this area; it was just another layer of purification required of me by the Lord. Now that we are both over the shock that the Lord is having me write about this area … let me start at the beginning.

The area of sexuality and pornography have never really been an area of struggle for me personally. As a teen, I had looked through inappropriate magazines on several occasions, but never felt drawn to them; it was more out of curiosity than desire. Once I was with a group of friends, mostly guys, and they put on a pornographic video. I was shocked but too embarrassed to leave. I mostly kept my head down.

In my teens and twenties, I periodically read the standard "romance novels" without thinking too much about it at the time, since they were readily available right out in the open on library shelves. (I have noticed my standards have changed considerably!) The graphic sex scenes in them, though shocking at first, soon just seemed to be acceptable, and not much different than what was emerging on the movie and television screens at the time. I did tend to make better choices with what I consumed in this area when I was on the upswing of my "on-again-off-again" walk with God. However, I am fairly certain even this level of exposure had a negative impact on my future choices in this area.

In my early stages of being a woman, I was never too concerned about my sexuality. It was definitely there; the crushes, desires and urges I experienced seemed similar to those around me, but it was not

Coming Through the Fire

something that controlled my life. It was part of life, but not life itself. Low-cut shirts exposing intimate parts of me were not what I considered comfortable, and I definitely did not want to "act sexy" to entice men. Yet I was not all pure either. I did have interactions with a few young men, but kept my virginity intact until I met my future husband.

During my marriage, however, it became another story. The whole area of sexuality became an underlying, all-consuming negative force in my life. The sexual pervasiveness and the attitudes held in our relationship, along with some bad choices, opened a door in my life that allowed for both extensive woundings and attacks on my sexuality and purity that would last for many years to come.

When I was first married, I believed my husband and I had a healthy sex-life. It seemed to be an area in which we did not fight, and both of us seemed more than satisfied. However, soon things with which I was not comfortable began to emerge and cause problems. At this point, I want to be direct in stating that the purpose of this chapter is not to detail what is appropriate or not in the sexual relationship between a husband and wife. That is between them and God. I don't even pretend to know. However, I do believe both partners must be comfortable with it, and it must not be coerced or forced. That is called rape, and yes, you can be raped by someone, even your husband or someone you have willingly had sex with previously. As well, sex in any way must not be used as a form of power or control over the other person. There are times when perfectly natural expectations of one partner may conflict with the comfort of the other if there has been a wounding in that area, but that will be dealt with in the following chapter.

Over the first few years, our seemingly healthy (as healthy as possible in an abusive relationship) sex-life eroded. When Rob first pulled out the pornographic magazines, I explained to him that they

Coming Through the Fire

made me feel uncomfortable. I couldn't help but think of what hurt the models so deeply for them to have made such a defiling life choice, and how it must be breaking their parents' hearts. "Besides," I'd say, "we don't need it. Everything is fine without it." The magazine would disappear, but occasionally resurface to once again test the waters.

Eventually, out came the adult videos. I offered up the same rationale, but this time it would be met with accusations of me being a prude, a cold fish and whatever other derogatory remarks he thought would hurt me enough to force me to concede. So, tired of fighting again, I surrendered my standards and allowed those images to infiltrate my mind and imprint on my subconscious.

What had once been a somewhat normal area of life was now wrought with confusion and soon began to engulf my life as it spilled out and overshadowed actions, attitudes and expectations in the marriage. Having not much experience in this area, I truly did not really know what normal sexuality should be like in a marriage relationship. Early on in dating, my wardrobe usually consisted of jeans, t-shirts and runners. As time passed, this came under fire, and I was encouraged to dress nicer, with runners, sweatpants and t-shirts belonging only in the gym. When I looked at this request from his point of view it seemed valid, and since it was so important to him, I made the concession and followed his dress code. This would have been fine if it stopped there. But during the marriage, his ever-mounting requests encouraged me to act completely out of my character. Some women are fine with wearing high heels when grocery shopping and around the house, but it is just not *me*. My daily wardrobe, what I wore under my clothes, and my choice of night attire became a source of agitation to him. I was constantly not up to his standards, and he did not hold back in letting me know this.

Coming Through the Fire

  I began to feel he would never be happy with me as me. I felt he just wanted a replica of one of the models from the magazines, or an actress from the x-rated videos. I was demanded to act sexier both in and out of the bedroom. I was constantly criticized for not taking on the role of *sex kitten*. Rob boldly suggested how great it would be if I underwent bust enhancement surgery. Soon everything was about sex, and his disappointment in me in that area loomed largely. I understand that men and women are wired differently in the area of sexuality, but this just seemed to border on the edge of insanity. I could not live up to his demands. And I definitely did not want to be forced to only play a fictitious role in my own life. I wanted my life to be my life, and not have to pretend to be someone else. I was being robbed of who I was.

  Needless to say, this became a huge area of contention between us. I no longer met his needs, which to me seemed to grow exceedingly insatiable. And as he was stripping more and more of my soul through the anger he unleashed on me and the constant abuse, it became harder and harder for me to be with him sexually at all. This, in turn, caused more problems, and sometimes ended in forced relations. When he was finished using me in this way, I would just cry ... my spirit broken and confused as to how my life could have turned out to be so sad.

  Many years later, I found myself still dealing with the aftermath of both my decisions and all that had happened to me because of the spiritual door they had opened in my life. The attacks of visual images I experienced from time to time, would sometimes be accompanied by strange sexual thoughts at the most inopportune times. As these attacks would happen, I would quickly take them to God, either by myself or with a highly trusted friend. Though it was embarrassing, I knew it was an attack and it had to be dealt with, both with repentance and asking the

Coming Through the Fire

Lord to cleanse me. Once I understood that the enemy can place thoughts in our minds, it was easier to deal with them and not feel ashamed.

Then one morning in my prayer time, after receiving prayer for both my first physical assault and the event where God protected me from date-rape (see "God's Protection" and The Letters on My Forehead" in *Break Forth*), I asked the Lord to give me clean hands and a pure heart. I asked Him to purify me and make me the gem He wished me to be, as was prophesied over me three days previous:

"The Father is also saying 'purity.' He is restoring purity to your whole being, and He is doing a purifying process, so you'll probably identify with what that means, how He is doing that body, soul and spirit ... He is purifying things in you. He is refining your heart and it is becoming a precious gem. It is like that is what He has always intended, for it to become this precious gem, so do not be afraid of the refining or the purifying process, because it is part of the work that He is doing in you."

In answer to that prayer, Holy Spirit led me through a purification process:

Oh, My beloved! Just rest in My presence. Be healed. My healing power flows through your body in rest. Feel Me as you breathe in clean air. My Spirit cleanses you, refreshes you, fills you. Breathe Me in. Let it fill every part of your being. Rest in Me. Be still and know that I work in stillness, in peace, in comfort. Trust. My hand is in yours. Feel Me. I was there, holding your hand, so close you

Coming Through the Fire

could feel my breath on you. Breathe in. Breathe out. Focus on Me. My grace is enough.

As I did what He asked, focusing on Him, breathing in and out, He led me to break off word curses spoken against me, and any other "thing" put on me by any of the men over my lifetime that had unholy sexual intentions toward me. Next, Holy Spirit asked me to break off and renounce any pictures, images, television shows, books, magazines, objects and movies I had been exposed to that intended to corrupt me or steal my purity. I had to tell any spiritual forces to leave, in Jesus' name, and any spiritual ties to be broken. I also had to break off the spirit of seduction.

As I did what the Lord was guiding me to do, I had a prophetic picture of little particles coming off of me and out of me and floating up and away. Then I felt a cold water washing over different parts of my body. It was only the third time I had felt this physical sensation connected to a spiritual event, and it was even more intense and lasted longer than ever before (into the next day), so it was quite a memorable, profound event in my life. The prophetic word I had received was more than confirmed that morning. Interestingly enough, the very next day I was directly attacked in this area once again. It happened through an encounter with Rob, where he spewed intensely descriptive sexual words at me. One more quick trip for prayer with a friend was all it took to wash me clean again.

As the Lord did His part in purifying me, He also required me to do my part. Music, books and television shows in which I once felt comfortable partaking, were no longer appropriate for my mind and

Coming Through the Fire

heart. Outwardly, many believers would not have an issue with these things, as they were only mildly suggestive of sexuality. However, as a now-single Christian female who was struggling to achieve and maintain sexual purity, they were off limits. Though I strongly believe in not partaking in anything sexually inappropriate, when you are not in a marriage relationship where you can express your sexual desires appropriately with your husband, it is that much more crucial to keep that which you take in with your eyes and allow into your imagination absolutely pure. Otherwise, it makes the battle for sexual purity that much more difficult.

As I kept drawing closer and closer to the Father, and as I kept a tight filter on what I allowed into my mind, these attacks subsided. Occasionally, I still wake up and remember a sexual dream and I have to pray to be washed clean of its effects on my mind. But that in itself is a victory, as it shows me the enemy can only infiltrate my mind when I am asleep. He no longer has access to it when I am awake and on guard!

Whether you are currently in a marriage relationship or not, God wants you to have a godly perspective of the human body, and view sexuality as He created and intended it to be. And this is entirely possible as we bring every area of our sexuality before Him with complete honesty and vulnerability. He knows it all anyway! Let's pray.

Oh Lord,

I come before You in complete honesty and vulnerability. I am grateful I can bring this sensitive area to You, confident You care about my purity and my pain. In Jesus' name I break off any enemy lies telling me right now that I cannot talk to You about this, telling me it is shameful, or that I am guilty or dirty. This area is much too heavy and important for me to carry on my own, so I give it to You. Be with me as I walk through it.

Please grant me the grace I need to accept any raw truth of my story that I need to accept and face. Holy Spirit, please minister to my spirit to bring the deliverance and healing I need. Place deep within me the knowledge that You will not only love and accept me, but You will treasure me, no matter what I have done, or what has been done to me.

Purity is no longer honored in many parts of society. But please help me to understand how honorable it is to You, and through Your mercy You will restore my purity and help me honor and desire it, as I lay it down before You. I come before You now and repent for the sins of _____. I renounce any books, pictures, magazines, movies, television shows, objects, dreams, actions, and any other things, attitudes, beliefs or ideas that have stolen my purity or have impacted me negatively in any way. In Jesus' name, I break every chain and every yolk of bondage that has kept me in sexual sin.

In Jesus' name, I cut off all unholy soul ties with any people with whom I have had any form of sexual relationship. I cut off every unholy soul tie I have had with any sexual object, belief or idea that has kept me in bondage. I declare I am free and I will walk in honor! Wash and cleanse me, Lord. Purify my mind and body. I ask for Your grace and wisdom to help me make wise choices in this area.

I close all doors of sexuality that are not pleasing to You. Please heal and seal all wounds I have in this area, and remove any trauma that is carried in my mind, emotions, and body. Restore the innocence and purity of my sexuality in all things.

Coming Through the Fire

Redeem me from all things that harm me sexually, known and unknown, things in which I have chosen, and those that have chosen me.

Lord, if I have used sex as a means of power and control over another, I ask You to show me. (Give time for Holy Spirit to reveal anything in this area. If anything is revealed, then take the time to repent.) Teach me healthy sexual boundaries. Bind up any confusion, in Jesus' name. I will walk in truth and freedom. Show me how to win the battle of sexual purity in all the specific circumstances of my life. (Give Holy Spirit time to give you strategies, and to show you specific things you need to do. Praying in your prayer language during this time helps to allow Him to reveal things, without your own brain getting involved!) Lord, release Your ministering angels to help in this fight, for me, my family and my friends.

Please give me a godly perspective of the human body. Help me view sexuality as You created it and intended it to be. Make me a reflection of Your glory—clean and sparkling, shiny and new—fully redeemed and washed in the blood of Jesus. Lord Jesus, help me hunger after You and after the purity You wish for us. Please open up Heaven's gates and rain down purity on me and on those around me, on my city, and my nation. Let the honoring of purity be passed down to our children. Let the beauty of sexuality, the way You intended it, be known across the land. I pray this in Jesus' name.

Coming Through the Fire

Who may climb the mountain of the LORD? Who may stand in his holy place? Only those whose hands and hearts are pure, who do not worship idols and never tell lies. They will receive the LORD'S blessing and have a right relationship with God their savior.

Psalm 24:3-5

And so, dear brothers and sisters, I plead with you to give your bodies to God because of all he has done for you. Let them be a living and holy sacrifice—the kind he will find acceptable. This is truly the way to worship him. Don't copy the behavior and customs of this world, but let God transform you into a new person by changing the way you think. Then you will learn to know God's will for you, which is good and pleasing and perfect.

Romans 12:1-2

So put to death the sinful, earthly things lurking within you. Have nothing to do with sexual immorality, impurity, lust, and evil desires.

Colossians 3:5a

Since you have heard about Jesus and have learned the truth that comes from him, throw off your old sinful nature and your former way of life, which is corrupted by lust and deception. Instead, let the Spirit renew your thoughts and attitudes. Put on your new nature, created to be like God—truly righteous and holy.

Ephesians 4:21-24

Coming Through the Fire

Why do You want us so clean, Lord?

I want to teach you things, show you things that need to be shared with others. To be close to Me, to be close to the heart of God, you need to be pure of heart. Clean hands, clean heart. You are washed in My grace, by My redemptive power. You need to know what it feels like to be fully redeemed, washed in My blood, pure for My purposes. Joy overflowing, sparkling water, reflections of My glory need to be seen when people look at you. They need to marvel at My healing power. They need to see you clean, see you glow so that they hunger after Me as you have. Experience My living waters. They flow through you, refreshing you, purifying you, making you precious in My sight ... pure, holy to shine forth for the world to see. Glorify Me. Glorify Me. Rest, and see what the Lord has done.

♥ Jesus

If you keep yourself pure, you will be a special utensil for honorable use. Your life will be clean, and you will be ready for the Master to use you for every good work. Run from anything that stimulates youthful lusts. Instead pursue righteous living, faithfulness, love, and peace. Enjoy the companionship of those who call on the Lord with pure hearts.

2 Timothy 2:21-22

Chapter II

Sexual Restoration

<u>Those Hands</u>

Those eyes … those eyes that look at me

So sweetly, making me believe I can do anything,

Be anything. They leave me breathless, those eyes.

Those lips … those lips that nuzzle up close and whisper

"I love you. I can't live without you."

Those lips, they touch my heart and bring life to

My soul.

And those hands … those hands that hold my hand

When times are tough, giving me the courage that *together*

We can make it through anything. Those hands make me think

Together we can take on the world and win.

Coming Through the Fire

And it is those same eyes that now rage with fire and burn my soul and those lips, those very lips now speak words of hate that kill my soul and still my heart and those hands those very same hands now pressed hard on my neck … it's those hands …

they leave me breathless.

And it is those hands, those very same hands
That pick up the pieces of the heart
The very same heart
Those very same hands
have shattered.

    It is a severe contrast—hands that heal versus hands that hurt; hands that make you feel afraid, ashamed and worthless. The touch of a hand should instill

    comfort   caring

        security   support

                deep calm …

                      peace.

YET SOMEHOW, INCOMPREHENSIBLY, SOMETIMES THAT UGLY CHOICE IS still made—using hands to callously kill—body and soul.

    After being wounded so deeply by hands that vowed to protect, it took years before I did not flinch at the touch of the hands of a man. At times, even with the genuine gestures of encouragement by the few men I trusted, I felt that uneasiness rise within my body. My mind would

Coming Through the Fire

struggle between frantically reassuring me that it was okay, and waiting for the ulterior motive of their touch to surface.

Over the years, trauma, big and small, deposited in me by unwanted and inappropriate touch, and angry, aggressive touch, without healing, had made me suspicious of all touch. I falsely believed still, that if a man was touching me, he wanted to use, abuse, or outright devour me. All touch is not sexual. All touch is not harmful or hurting. All touch does not strip you of all security and leave you feeling ravaged, vulnerable, raw—exposed, beaten and bruised. That should never be, never should have been.

Touch should elicit the feeling of someone standing right beside you in life, partnering with you, supporting you. It should build you up, make you feel loved, secure and able to conquer all of life's challenges. I had to relearn this truth. And I know, some of you reading this right now, will have to relearn this truth. I speak to those of you who were torn down in every aspect of your being, unsupported, used and abused, left to shoulder the entire load and more on your bare back; stumbling, falling and kicked in the stomach when you were down, literally or figuratively. You have learned, to the core of your being, to mistrust and to fear; to always expect something bad to get you. Because it did. So many, many times.

I speak to those of you who have been intimidated with hands that threatened harm, though not actually touched, and to you who have had those angry eyes cut into you while that voice, hissing or thundering, it matters not, terrorized you. You too have had the trauma and fear bled into your soul that can breed fear and mistrust of touch. Do not minimize what happened to you. Threats alone, verbal and nonverbal, are physical violence and can alter who God intended you to be.

Coming Through the Fire

I speak to you who have been hit or beaten, molested or raped. The pain goes deep. The anguish is real. It haunts you in the night. It has changed you, body and mind. You may have found it difficult to fully function or engage in a godly sex life with your husband. It perhaps has destroyed all hopes of a healthy relationship with a man. It may even have altered your sexual identity. You may have vowed to never again let a man touch you, hurt you.

All of you have been robbed of so, so much. My soul hurts to think of all you have gone through. Right now, the hands of a man may be a symbol of anxiety, of harm, of hatred. You fear the touch of hands. You fear the touch of the Father's hands. Even *His hands* make you tremble in fear, cowering like you had been forced to do so before.

But layer by layer, gently, the Lord wants to heal your pain as you give it to Him. He wants to restore you. He wants to restore you mentally, emotionally and physically. He wants to restore to you a healthy sexuality. He will walk with you and cry with you. He will shoulder the load. He will hear your cries. He wants to restore the security in the touch of His hand. He wants to show you His hand means sacrifice

safety love

grace mercy

healing freedom.

You can trust feeling His touch. Hands are not about force or threat. Hands are not about fear or lust. He will wash you clean. He wants to heal all your wounds so you can enter into a healthy, intimate sexual relationship with your marriage partner. He wants to heal any unhealthy areas in your sex life that are hindering the godly intimacy you have or will have with your husband. As hard as this is to deal with, do not be ashamed. There is no shame in taking this intimate area to the

Coming Through the Fire

Lord. He knows it all anyway. He loves you so much and wants you healthy, whole and fully alive, in every area of your being, sexuality included.

So come, let me walk with you, cry with you, as you pray with us. As you risk vulnerability and hand it over to the One who restores, He will set you free. Take a deep breath. Exhale. Here we go.

> **Prophetic word - October 2014**
>
> Have you seen the movie *Brave Heart*? I am so happy the Lord spoke about *Brave Heart* today because when I think of *Brave Heart*, I see the other half of the victory was the romance he was fighting for the whole time. And I feel today it has been spoken over you. God wants to import romance into your spirit today. As He is bringing you forth, beauty from ashes, He is raising you up, instilling in you that beauty. There is so much in Song of Songs I believe is for you. It is like that intimacy with the Lord as you are speaking to Him and He is speaking to you, and the knowing in your spirit, the intimacy, the romance with the Lord God. And I just want to speak these words. I want you to believe, in Jesus' name: "How beautiful you are, my darling. Oh, how beautiful. Your eyes are like doves." God is continually gazing upon you as you gaze upon Him. And He is saying to you today, "How beautiful you are, my darling, my darling." I pray these words go deep into my sister today, deep into my sister. "How beautiful you are, my darling."

Coming Through the Fire

Dear Lord,

    Thank You that You are faithful to heal and comfort me. Thank You that You want to soothe the scars that are carried on the most tender parts of my body and soul. Lord, anywhere my identity was stolen because of unholy attitudes and actions in the sexual realm on my part, or on the part of others, I ask for redemption and restoration, and for healing of all trauma it has inflicted upon me. Please remove the veil of shame off of my eyes so I can see You for who You are—my Redeemer, and so I can accept myself as You have made me to be, in my true form and identity, not the counterfeit one with which the enemy has tried to mask me. I break off the mocking spirit and I cancel its attempts to bring deception or distraction.

    Help me to be who You originally designed me to be in all areas, including sexuality. In Jesus' name, I break off anything sexually inappropriate that was deposited on me by anyone over my lifetime. I break off any curse words spoken over me in the area of sexuality, and any words I've spoken over myself or others, by the power of the cross and the shed blood of Jesus. I cancel any vows I've made about sexuality and sexual identity. Lord, if there is a specific vow I have made, such as "I will never let a man touch me or hurt me again," or "I will never trust a man," please reveal it to me. (Give Holy Spirit time to reveal any vows you have personally made. If any are revealed, then cancel them, and speak the opposite.) I come out of agreement that _____. I will instead, _____.

Coming Through the Fire

I ask You, Lord, to push back the oppression that has been spoken into existence from the words spoken by the generations when they believed the lies of the enemy that have twisted and confused Your true creation of love and sex. Show them the truth of love, intimacy and sexuality as You originally created them to be. Please bring people into my life that will love and honor me in the ways You intended relationships to be, and teach those ones currently in my life what it means to love as You love. But Lord, I give You permission to remove them if they refuse to walk in this. Help me walk away from all things that do not bring honor to Your name, Lord Jesus.

Lord, when You were whipped across the face, You took the blame for us. I thank You for that, so I no longer have to blame myself or others for anything I have done or that has been done to me. Lord, You take the blame, and in that, the victory was won. Thank You for that, Lord. I release and forgive those who hurt me, knowing that they are in Your hands to deal with, and understanding that this releases me to heal. Without my release of forgiveness to them, as hard as this is, I cannot heal. I do this in obedience and ask You to make in real in my heart. Thank You for washing me clean and white as snow. I am pure in Your eyes. I am beautiful. I am appreciated. I am loved. I am treasured and cherished. I am fully restored and found worthy in Your sight, by the blood of the Lamb. Thank You, My Lord. I pray this in the precious name of Jesus Christ of Nazareth.

Coming Through the Fire

How beautiful you are, my darling, how beautiful!
Your eyes are like doves.
Song of Songs 1:15

My lover said to me, "Rise up, my darling! Come away with me, my fair one! Look, the winter is past, and the rains are over and gone. The flowers are springing up, the season of singing birds has come, and the cooing of turtledoves fills the air. The fig trees are forming young fruit, and the fragrant grapevines are blossoming. Rise up, my darling! Come away with me, my fair one!"
Song of Songs 2:10-13

You have captured my heart, my treasure, my bride. You hold it hostage with one glance of your eyes, with a single jewel of your necklace. Your love delights me, my treasure, my bride. Your love is better than wine, your perfume more fragrant than spices.
Song of Songs 4:9-10

Coming Through the Fire

O My dear, dear One

My heart breaks over you, my wounded one. KNOW how I see you. FEEL how I see you—how I love you. KNOW I see every part of your pain. I will heal you as you draw near. Come, sit with Me, stay with Me. I ease your pain, your heart. I fill it with My grace, My power. It will be sufficient as you press into Me, as you let Me pick up the pieces of your heart. I will create a new thing, not restore the old. It will be a new thing, a glorious thing. I draw you into My arms and hold you, as one would hold a delicate flower, in awe of its every detail. My tender mercies seek to revive you; seek to restore you. As hard as it is to expose all that lies buried in the deepest part of you, locked behind the walls, know your secrets are safe with Me as you confess them to Me. It is then, when you give them to Me, that I can take them, remove them from your heart so they no longer pierce like the jagged, metal edges that have been ravaging you for so long. Let them go. All of them. Give them to Me. I can carry them like no other. Trust Me, My Sweet One.

♥Jesus

Chapter 12

Walking Through the Grief

Journal Entry - April 2015

I come to you, Lord, with empty hands and an open heart to receive abundant blessing. I am needy. My life path has been difficult and I am drained of strength. Thank You for filling me with Your presence, You in me, and me in You. Thank You that Your power flows into weak ones aware of our need for You.

Coming Through the Fire

WHEN YOU LIVE IN OR HAVE LIVED IN AN ABUSIVE SITUATION, THINGS emerge that are somewhat problematic in reconciling between your heart and the logical part of your brain. No matter how hard the situation was in which you have lived (or continue to live) you still will grieve all you have lost, whether you have left the situation or not.

Though some believe I left my marriage of my own free will and therefore should not have anything to be sad about, I was more so forced into this *choice*. Absolutely convinced I was on a path full speed to destruction—emotionally, mentally and physically—I did what I believed I had to do to save what was left of me and my family. The logical part of my brain knows this choice of leaving was the only one that had remained. After the many years and attempts at other plausible solutions to the ever-growing violence in my relationship, I knew with all that was within me, I had exhausted every possible avenue to healing and restoring my marriage. The longer we continued to live within the same walls, the further down this path I would venture, and the longer and harder it would be to heal. My brain knew that when I left, it was my only chance for survival. It was the only way I could begin to heal the many layers of trauma I had suffered, without more being inflicted on me faster than I could heal. There was really no other choice to take the foot of the oppressor off my neck than to get out from under the same roof. With all that being said, one would have believed I would have absolutely nothing to be sad about; nothing at all to grieve. Or so I thought.

Here it was, seven years later, and while my brain was screaming "Freedom!" there was still no song or dance in my soul. It was almost as if my heart had been numb for so long, but now that the trauma was being removed from my mind and body, it too, was being revived, only to discover its ache. If I was now able to walk in freedom and was

Coming Through the Fire

receiving my healing for which I had been so ferociously fighting, why was my heart suffocating in such deep sorrow? Hard to reconcile …

But the Lord showed me that like in any death or loss, one has to grieve. One has to walk through the deep sorrow of loss—any loss—feeling its shards, like glass, piercing into the tender parts of your soul. Good and bad, I still needed to grieve all I had lost. I had to grieve the loss of my family life as it was when times were good. I had to grieve the loss of my hopes, dreams and expectations for what I at one time believed would be my life. The life I now lived had not been a part of my life plans, not even remotely.

I had to grieve the loss of my marriage. Though there was more bad than good, I still had to accept that loss. I had to let go of having a stable, two-parent environment in which my kids could grow up. Though this had never been a reality in the situation we were in, the hope and expectation for it, and therefore its loss, still had to be grieved. I had to grieve what never was.

I even had to grieve the loss of my husband. As hard as that is to process, I still had to grieve the loss of him to some degree; who he was, all of him. Deep in my spirit, I understood He is a child of God, just like me, who has walked through hell on so many levels, and this grieves God. And so it grieves me. I had to let go of the hope that perhaps "one day he would change, things would get better." I am not saying he will never change. Anything is possible with God. But I had to let go of it; no longer bet my life on it. I had to grieve it so I could finally leave it fully in the Lord's hands. I even had to grieve my loss of the *status of married*. I had been single for so long previously and had not enjoyed it in my latter years. Being married gave me the ideology of being accepted; someone had chosen *me* as the one with whom to walk life's path. I hated having to check off the *divorced* box on forms. Though I no longer feel the deep rejection that once brought about, and I now believe I am absolutely accepted and chosen by the Lord Himself—He is my husband—I still don't like that little box!

So as hard as it is to comprehend, I had to grieve all I had lost in what was a dangerous, volatile marriage. I had to feel all of its pain. I had to allow myself time to be sad; to grieve. I had to walk through the sorrow and keep giving it to the Lord. I had to keep surrendering the loneliness the sorrow evoked. But then I had to refocus on the Lord and all I had gained in my new life, in what I was learning and how I was growing. I had to walk past the time of grief, and start rejoicing in the Lord. I had to let go of all the sorrow deep in my heart when He called and said, "It is time."

I still go back there once in a while. Thoughts of grief and sadness will rise up to the surface from somewhere deep inside of me, triggered by some seemingly insignificant event. And again I have to allow myself to feel the pain and walk through it. Once I recognize something as grief, I briefly explore it, talking about it with a trusted friend, or journaling, and then praying. I surrender it to the Lord for Him to carry. Sometimes it is difficult to recognize the feelings, as grief. It can disguise itself as anger, fear, frustration, anxiety, or depression. It can steal motivation before it is even exposed as grief. It can cause physical symptoms of weakness, fatigue, heaviness, among others. It can stir up headaches and bellyaches. It can give one the desire to isolate, to put oneself into a little box, and not have to keep on living in the outside world, or at all. It can be a dangerously slippery slope; one in which the enemy will take advantage of if you begin to dwell on it day after day. It can threaten to take you back to a place of discouragement, depression and despair if it is not released.

Coming Through the Fire

Healing from grief does not necessarily mean you will completely forget about your loss, whatever that loss is for you. It does mean, however, that it no longer constantly consumes you to the point of not functioning. It means joy can be restored to your life. It means you are ready to delve into the new, exciting things God has promised you. It means you recognize that a life focused on grief is not what the Lord has for you. He wants to lift you up. He raises your chin and helps you look to Him. He gazes at you as you gaze at Him. And He sees you. Day by day, He restores your joy, strengthens and encourages you as you seek Him. He will place amazing people all around you to walk with you, link shields with you, as you ask. He wants you to know you are fully loved, accepted and chosen. You are His beloved. You can now walk with your head held high, meeting the challenges thrown at you head on, full of confidence of one who walks in the presence of the Lord. Let's pray.

Dear Lord God,

Creator of all in Heaven and on Earth, thank You that eye has not seen, ear has not heard the things You have prepared for those who love You. How much more You want for us than for us to feel overwhelmed, consumed and grieved by the sorrows of this world.

Lord, in times of my despair, my pain, my hurt ... I just want my heart to stop bleeding. That seems to be the limit of vision I can hold for my life. But You see so much more than that for me. You are calling me out of the desolate places and drawing me into the fertile valleys. You are calling me out of the place of grief and darkness and brokenness. You want to make me strong. You want to give me the heart of a warrior to transform not only my life but the lives of those around me.

Coming Through the Fire

Thank You that joy comes in the morning. I surrender my grieving heart unto You, and ask You to heal it, renew it, and restore the joy within. Help me dare to hope again. Breathe Your life back into me. Thank You for Your resurrection power that brings me up from the ashes of defeat and makes beauty of all the ugliness and sadness in my life.

I bind up the powers of darkness that have brought death and destruction into my life and that of those I care about, and I declare that through the power of Christ, they will not bring me down, or take me out! I bind up and throw down every spirit of paralyzing depression and grief that is casting its shadow on me. Jesus, raise me up, stronger than ever, ready to engage in every assignment You give me and obey every commandment You lay before me, working everything in my life for good—and that includes my grief and my pain.

You have collected every one of my tears in a bottle, and I ask You now to overturn that bottle onto the dry ground of my heart and those hurting hearts around me. Cause them to flourish and bear good fruit. I speak life, joy and peace over each one. Bring the song back into our hearts, Father God!

Lord, if grief is the unrecognized source of any of my thoughts, behaviors or actions, please reveal this to me, and guide me in giving it all to You. I bind up any stress that has come in with my grief, or that has prevented me from fully walking through the grieving process. Please heal every part of my body that has been negatively impacted by the physical effects of stress and grief. Release every bit of trauma and grief being held anywhere in my body. Fill every place with Your healing oil.

Coming Through the Fire

Thank You for those around me who have supported me in difficult situations. This is a testament to Your faithfulness. You know what I need. No matter where I go or what I go through, I am not separated from You; Your hand is always upon me.

Lord, I ask You to turn the scars of my deep pain, now healed, into compassion so I can comfort others wallowing in the deep throes of grief. Help me to share the strength You have given to me with others. Help me to walk in victory in every aspect of my life, in the full authority You grant me as Your child. Help me to bring healing and encouragement through the power of Holy Spirit to the ones You place around me.

Help me to praise You in spite of circumstance—even in awful circumstances and for awful circumstances because with each trial of fire comes Your mercy, grace and glory. I thank You for the spiritual authority the tribulations You have allowed in my life have brought me. Grow my trust in You as I walk through each of these times of fire. Purify me. Sanctify me. Refine me through the fire. Help me draw close to You so I can know You more. I pray this in the precious name of Jesus Christ. Amen.

Coming Through the Fire

I will never forget this awful time, as I grieve over my loss. Yet I still dare to hope when I remember this: The faithful love of the LORD never ends! His mercies never cease. Great is his faithfulness; his mercies begin afresh each morning. I say to myself, "The LORD is my inheritance; therefore, I will hope in him!" The LORD is good to those who depend on him, to those who search for him.
Lamentations 3:20-25

"Look, God's home is now among his people! He will live with them, and they will be his people. God himself will be with them. He will wipe every tear from their eyes, and there will be no more death or sorrow or crying or pain. All these things are gone forever."
Revelation 21:3b-4

He heals the brokenhearted and bandages their wounds.
Psalm 147:3

My flesh and my heart fail;
But God is the strength of my heart and my portion forever.
Psalm 73:26 (NKJV)

God blesses those who mourn, for they will be comforted.
Matthew 5:4

Coming Through the Fire

Dear Child,

    I will direct your path. I will fill you with joy. Keep dancing before Me. You are still in a season of grieving, learning and growing. The grief will soon pass. You are grieving all you have lost. But soon you will focus on all you have gained in this. The time is here to rejoice in Me. Let go of all the sorrow deep in your heart. You are still hanging on to it. You are walking through your sorrow. Feel it, but keep walking through it.

I still feel such a deep sadness, Lord.

Give it to Me.

I feel so alone, Lord. It is either rush rush with the kids, or totally alone.

I will lift you up. I will raise your chin and you will look to Me. I gaze at you. I see you.

                                      ♥Love Jesus

Coming Through the Fire

Author's note:

Grieving is a natural process that everyone has to go through as they encounter loss in their lives. But the enemy can also use it against you to deter and stop you cold from walking out all God has for you. It can become so big it overtakes you, engulfs you, seemingly swallowing up all the Lord has done for you, and the healing works you have already experienced in your life. But it does not have to be so. There are entire books written on this process, and people specifically trained to guide you through it. If you find yourself struggling greatly in this area, please seek adequate counsel. As deep as grief goes, there is healing grace that comes from your heavenly Father as you seek Him. You will be restored.

Chapter 13

Receiving God's Love

> If someone says, "I love God," but hates a fellow believer, that person is a liar; for if we don't love people we can see, how can we love God, whom we cannot see? And he has given us this command: Those who love God must also love their fellow believers.
>
> 1 John 4:20-21

I STRUGGLE WITH RECEIVING. THE OTHER DAY, A DEAR FRIEND ASKED what I wanted to do for my birthday. She offered to have me and some other friends to her place for lunch. My response was a non-committal, lame comment: "I don't know…" The next day the Lord asked me to accept her gracious offer. I had to force myself to do so, and restrain from ending with those types of words that suggest she needn't bother. The very next day, when I asked the Lord about what He wanted me to

Coming Through the Fire

share with you as I wrote about receiving God's love, He whispered only one word: the name of my friend.

She was God's hands, showing me love and assuring me the Lord saw me that day. I was humbled. By rejecting what she wanted to do for me, I was rejecting God's love. If our own walls of protection block us from receiving from others and receiving without conditions, we have also unknowingly, though successfully kept out the love, mercy, and grace God is so freely offering us. Opening our heart and receiving from others is a step toward being open enough to receive from God. He wants amazing blessings to be poured out over us, and people are His hands and feet.

All throughout the Word, he exhorts Christians to love other people, those who believe, and those who do not. I believe the other half of the mandate would be for us to receive that love He has directed His messengers to bestow on us, or why else would it be so important to show His love? It is okay to receive! It is more than okay. The Lord wants it for you, especially you who constantly put yourself at the bottom of the pile. Your heart may never seem to be the priority. Like those last few items of laundry in a basket continually buried by other reoccurring articles, your heart rarely seems to be the most pressing issue. There is always something more important to do, someone more needy, someone worse off than you ... and so your heart sits, numb from disuse, maybe slightly hardened or jaded—it had to be because of all you've been through—waiting to be resurrected. But now is the time to dig down to the bottom of the dirty laundry pile and uncover your heart. Let it be fully exposed to the cleansing power of Holy Spirit, so it can fully receive all the love God has for you.

And this love is magnificent. It is tremendous. I have felt it, and it almost knocked me over. We are not able to feel it all the time, or we

Coming Through the Fire

wouldn't be able to or even want to function in daily life ... but I know it, believe it and have felt it physically.

Even before my heart was open and able to receive the great love God has for me, He showed me what it felt like, through revealing His love for another. It was absolutely overwhelming. This remarkable event occurred at a camp meeting. In the middle of worship, as I looked at one of the worship leaders, (she was wearing a yellow t-shirt—I remember it vividly) I felt this incredible sensation sweep over me. It moved me to instant tears—weeping, actually. I had to sit down. I was completely undone.

I knew what I was feeling was God's love for this woman. There was nothing like it. It came over me like a wave. He then downloaded a prophetic love letter from Him, for me to give to her. After reading His sweet words to her, her hug and tears assured me she had received His word and His love. She left me with a promise that one day she would tell me her story.

This was not to be the only time I felt radically changed by a direct encounter with God's love. It also happened during worship one Sunday—I don't even remember the context or the song or the words that led me to this thought process. But suddenly, I was picturing God as He watched His Son on the cross, in agony, hanging from spikes through His flesh. He had to turn His head to look away so He could go through with what He knew must happen. At one time, I had callously thought, *It wouldn't be so bad ... God knew Jesus would be resurrected again and be seated beside Him on the throne.* But suddenly I imagined my son, my only son, up there on the cross, suffering, bleeding, dying—fully able to help him, yet knowing that must not happen ... and yes, even knowing I would see Him again ... it MADE NO DIFFERENCE. I finally understood the

Coming Through the Fire

depth of God's unimaginable love for us. I thanked Him for it, and I fully received it.

Some time later, I asked God to show me how much He loved me. I expected a picture of rainbows and butterflies, or at least kittens or some other soft, fuzzy thing. He showed me ... an iceberg! I laughed. Typical God move to not give the expected! But I knew it spoke to the fact that there is more depth to His love than we can see, know, or even possibly understand. It is unexplored, uncharted terrain ... a mystery that will keep us intrigued for time and all eternity. I look forward to realizing it more and more each day.

And now my commission is to partner with God to help others, to help you, heal your heart so you can fully receive His amazing love, mercy and grace. And then you can live in hope, peace and joy. But it doesn't stop there. Once you can receive and be filled with God's love, you can begin to overflow with it. It is from this overflow of His love poured into you that you can truly and deeply reach out and love others without reserve. (Not without boundaries—without reserve, but I'm sure that will be another chapter somewhere down the line!)

In this love we can be the hands and feet of God, and love others with a tender heart as He would have us love them. It is in this love that we can see others as He sees them, as they are, and as they are called to be. The Lord loves His people with a compassion beyond all reason. He needs people to love one another to the depths of *His* soul, too. His heart breaks for all His children, those who trust Him and those who don't. He needs our heart to break for all His children as well—especially the lost and the hurting. In this love we can encourage them, build them up, and help them grow strong.

And He loves you as much as He loves each of His people. His love washes over you every day anew. As He washes you with His love,

Coming Through the Fire

He strengthens you to walk in His love for His people. He will teach you to walk in His love, with your heart breaking, yet still full of peace and joy. This seems impossible from a human perspective, but nothing is impossible with God. He is God of all things in the world and out of the world, physical and spiritual—those things you can touch and those things that can touch you.

It is this all-encompassing love that provides part of the armor that protects us as He calls us to fight the battles on the front lines. Without it, we have no purpose. Without it, there is no fight; no reason to fight. Are you ready? Do you want to find the parts of your heart buried beneath the rubble—those parts you need to release to God—so you can receive from Him and from others? Let's pray.

Dear Heavenly Father,

Creator of everything, everywhere, who am I that You are mindful of me? Yet You know me intimately and love me with a heart that never changes. Thank You for loving me. I am sorry for all the ways I have rejected Your love. I ask You to break down all the walls of protection I have constructed that attempt to keep out Your love and the love of others—Your hands and feet. Open my heart, O Lord, and help me to receive all of Your love, and all You have for me. I receive the blessings You pour over me.

I give You all of my heart—the buried parts, the hidden parts, the shattered parts—all of it, to do with it as You wish. Soften my heart, O God, heal and restore all the areas of it that have become jaded or were wounded through the trials of life. Fill it with Your healing balm. Resurrect it, Lord!

Coming Through the Fire

Let me tangibly feel Your love wash over me! Show me how You love me. I give You permission to make me undone with Your love and the love You have for others. I ask for that same love to flow forth from my own heart onto others, far and near. Let this love allow me to see them as You see them. Let my heart break for Your children as Your own heart does. Let love flow from me so they may be built up, encouraged and made strong. Change me through the power of Your love! Clothe me with the armor of Your love. Let me understand its depth more each day. Let Your love bring the peace and joy, courage and hope I need in my life to carry me through those times that seem overwhelming.

Father God, I ask for a revelation of what You went through, and what Your Son went through with the death on the cross, so I have a deep appreciation of Your sacrifices and Your love for us, for me. Let that revelation permeate my being so I am ever changed; so it will be reflected in all my thoughts and actions. I accept the forgiveness His shed blood brings to me, and the righteousness it grants me in the eyes of the Father.

Heal and seal this work in me, Lord. I pray this in the lovely name of Jesus Christ.

Coming Through the Fire

For this is how God loved the world: He gave his one and only Son, so that everyone who believes in him will not perish but have eternal life. God sent his Son into the world not to judge the world, but to save the world through him.
John 3:16-17

Dear friends, let us continue to love one another, for love comes from God. Anyone who loves is a child of God and knows God. But anyone who does not love does not know God, for God is love. God showed us how much he loved us by sending his one and only Son into the world so that we might have eternal life through him. This is real love—not that we loved God, but that he loved us and sent his Son as a sacrifice to take away our sins. Dear friends, since God loved us that much, we surely ought to love each other. No one has ever seen God. But if we love each other, God lives in us, and his love is brought to full expression in us.
1 John 4:7-12

Coming Through the Fire

Dear Child,

Open up to receive My love. Open up to receive all I have for you. Be open to My Spirit. It is gentle and soft, not forceful. I am not an angry God. Enjoy your time with Me. Stay soft before Me to receive My love. Feel it wash over you. Let your body relax under My love. Feel My love. Receive My love. Take away that hard edge of resistance and give in to My gentle grace, mercy and love that I have for you. You have not yet known My love. Receive it. Do not be afraid of love. My love is soft and gentle as the sweet spring rain falling softly around you. It fills you with peace and life and does not harm you. Love was never meant to harm you, bruise you, but to care for you and tend your wounds, not create them.

O My Little One, My heart is so fond of you in all ways. It holds you, it caresses your face, soft and gently. It will not harm. Harsh words will not spill out of My lips to harm you, nor provoke you. My words are tender. My mercies are flowing over you. I love you with all My heart. Enter into a love relationship with Me, and I will teach you how to love others, and be soft and gentle. Let your guard down, o Little One. I will take care of you.

♥Love Jesus

Chapter 14

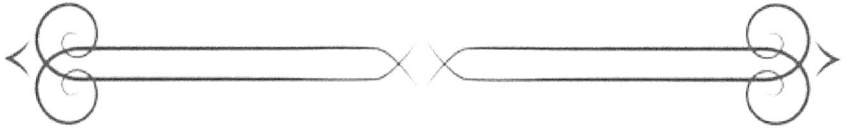

Inheritance Word

October 5, 2013

"Be strong and courageous, for you are the one who will lead these people to possess all the land I swore to their ancestors I would give them. Be strong and very courageous. Be careful to obey all the instructions Moses gave you. Do not deviate from them, turning either to the right or to the left. Then you will be successful in everything you do. Study this Book of Instruction continually. Meditate on it day and night so you will be sure to obey everything written in it. Only then will you prosper and succeed in all you do. This is my command—be strong and courageous! Do not be afraid or discouraged. For the LORD your God is with you wherever you go."

Joshua 1:6-9

THIS IS THE LIFE-CHANGING INHERITANCE WORD I RECEIVED FROM A total stranger at a Bible study one night. At that time I was still healing and did not see myself as a leader of anyone at all; I was just getting back on my feet. But it was my first hint there was more to me than I believed and more to my life than I had experienced. I finally dared to believe God had a purpose for me—for all the fire I had been through in my life.

Coming Through the Fire

It deeply impacted me, but it would be over a year before I would start really pressing into the Lord.

I will let my journals tell the story. They tell it best, reflecting the dialogue between the Lord and I as we spent intimate time together in the secret place of my prayer closet. He revealed His love for me and His people (of which you are one), His plans for me, and He gave me encouragement, direction and instruction. My side of the entries are predominantly a prayer; my life and heart poured out to the Lord. As you read, I pray it becomes your prayer as well, for you too, are called to high places, to be a warrior fighting on the front lines, leading the charge. Read it as such—a prayer from your own heart, adapting and expanding it as you are led by Holy Spirit so it becomes your own. My Joshua commission too, then becomes your commission, if you choose to accept. Have no fear. You will be well trained.

Coming Through the Fire

February 28, 2015

 Share your journey with others. Teach them how you love Me. Show them how you hear My voice. I will lead you then, as I lead you now. Do not worry, it is not you, it is Me who will lead and guide them through you. It is My voice they will hear, not yours. It is My responsibility, not yours. I have created them, I love them, I am forming them and conforming them to what I have for them. It is not your plan. I have plans for each one of them, and they will hear My voice to them through your journey, through your struggles. I have released this writing in you. I will release their gifts, each one their own, in them, for their journey. I need you to hear My voice in all you do.

 I am your strength and shield, but also your wisdom and knowledge. I know things you know nothing of, but I will reveal some of it to you as you are obedient to Me, and follow My voice and bidding. You will hear My voice, as they will. All who are ready to hear will hear. They are My people, and I am their God. It is time for all to open their hearts to their God, and see the wonderful treasures in store for those who love Me. I am the treasure. All will find when they seek. Get ready. It will be quite a ride.

Love Jesus

March 2, 2015

    Thank You, Father, for what You are doing in me and through me. I am excited about the adventure You have put me on. Please keep expanding me, and opening the doors that You want to be opened. Your will, Lord, Your agenda.

    Thank You for the abundant life You offer to everyone who turns to You. Thank You for filling me with Your life. Thank You for blessing me with more and more joy and abundant life. I invite You to fully live in me.

I feel like I am supposed to take the prophetic class. Please confirm that and open up that opportunity if that is Your will.

Coming Through the Fire

My Child,

You need more training. I am training you up for exciting things. Do what you are doing. Follow My leading voice. Take the steps I have put before you. Walk in My light. Walk in My love. Walk out your destiny. I will give you the love, the grace, the patience, the time and all the resources that you need. Be obedient. Hear My voice. Hear My calling. I am calling you to a high purpose. Yours and yours alone.

March 2, 2015

I received a prophetic word at a prayer session tonight. It was strong and powerful. I was called to set captives free. It more than confirmed the calling I had been feeling in my heart for the previous month.

March 3, 2015

Wow! Wow! Wow! Wow! It is all true! I am hearing Your voice! Thank You sooo much for confirming it in all Barry's prophetic word! I am humbled and awed at the mantle You have placed on me. Help me be patient. Help me grow into the person You are calling and needing me to be. It is awesome ... it is amazing. Wow! Wow! Wow! So many exciting things happening. Your path is exciting and amazing.

I pray for continued healing and hearing of Your voice, guiding steps, and no fear as I continue my journey. I am so humbled and in awe of You! Thank You for loving me. Teach me to discern Your voice. Holy Spirit, please give me the gift of discernment. Please reveal and develop my other gifts. Help me walk closely with You each moment, listening to Your directives and enjoying Your companionship. Help me walk out my destiny. Go before me in all I do.

Help me to be the person You are calling me to be, in all areas. Wow! I so delight in You, Lord! I am so blown away!!! I am overwhelmed and overtaken by Your calling. But I am yours. I do not fear. I put my trust in You. Show me. Lead me. Guide me. I am Yours, fully Yours. Not my will, but Yours. Thank You for Your confirmation! You have called me ... I accept.

Coming Through the Fire

(God Speaks)

You hear My voice. Now can you stop doubting? The chains of doubt are gone. I will flow through you. Have no fear. That is not your portion. I will lead and guide you, each word, one at a time. Do not look ahead. I will be on the path with you. Do not try to figure it out, as I have told you. I will confirm each step you take, as I need to. I will show you the journey one step at a time, one word at a time, one letter at a time, as I have planned. You are not on this journey alone. I still surround you with My shield, My armor, My people who love Me. You are not on your own. I have placed people all around you; strong people. They will help you. You are still in My shield of protection. No harm will come to you. Your trust is in Me. It will not waver. You will waver <u>no</u> more. <u>No</u> more will you <u>doubt</u>. No more will you <u>fear</u>. No more will you be scared to take each step that I place in front of you.

Coming Through the Fire

You are strong in Me. You are wise in Me. I will allow you to discern. You do know My voice. Put rest to your doubts. Put silence to your fear. You do hear My voice and you are hearing My voice. All is well. Trust. Depend. Hope in Me. Still keep your eyes on Me, and stay still until I tell you to move. I will give you directions and guidance, and confirm all I tell you. Look for it. Know it. Believe it. Keep sharing your heart. You know it is true. It was all for a reason, My reason, My plan for you; My plan of grace and perfection. You are who you need to be. You will be who you need to be. You will see.

Treasure My song to you always. Pursue Me as you have. Keep your eyes focused only on Me. Do not get distracted. Get out of the boat but keep your eyes fixed hard on Me. You are Mine. I am yours. You are My beloved and I will take care of you through this. Love Me as I love you.

Love Jesus

March 4, 2015

Thank You for giving me such a high calling. Thank You for calling me to be a warrior. I accept, and I am honored. Please show me and train me. Open up the heavens over me and send Your power down so I can be a worthy warrior.

Lord, keep me from the temptation of being anxious. Keep me in continual communication with You. Please help me keep my heart thankful. Keep me aware of Your presence. Keep filling me with Your light, peace, hope, joy and power. Show me my problems, the problems of this world, from Your perspective. Lord, keep me from hypocrisy. Help me acknowledge You and proclaim You every time You ask, and more. Thank You, Holy Spirit, for teaching me what to say when I need it.

Increase my faith, O Lord. Thank You for caring so much for me.

You have done so many wondrous things in my life. Keep my treasure as You, my family, my friends and Your people. Keep me ready for Your return at all times. Thank You that I am a child of the light and don't belong in the dark. Thank You for protecting me with the armor of faith and love. Thank You for the vision You gave my friend of me in incredible, beautiful, strong heavenly armor. I ask too, for that revelation and vision. I ask You to show me, in situations, what is happening in the spiritual realm. Thank You for the helmet of confidence of our salvation.

Thank You for all my giftings. I hand them to You and ask for You to help me develop them. Use them in me, bring them out. Let me help others with them. Thank You for all You are showing, and the power You have released in my life. Keep showing me the steps to take. Let me hear Your voice, and block out all other voices.

Dear Child,

Be as one crying in the wilderness. Hear My voice. Hear My cry. I am with you. I walk beside you and you do hear My voice. I ask you to do these things in My name. Not in your name; not in your power but by the power of the Holy Spirit. The Spirit will be released in you more and more as you obey Me, and hear My voice. I give you the power you need to do all I ask; no more, no less. I am the power you seek. I am the treasure you seek. I am yours. You are mine. We walk together in this, side by side, hand in hand. I am your strength and your justification. All you have is Mine. Now I can work in you. I can release all you have within you, for My glory. You have submitted your heart to Me. It is Mine and I cherish it. The Holy Spirit wind has cleansed you and will keep cleansing you as you seek Me out in the quietness of your heart.

Coming Through the Fire

Be Mine in all you think, all you say, all you do. Record all the things I have asked you to do. Make notes of your journey. It is for sharing. You will share your walk with Me. It is for all to see My power. My glory will shine in your life. It will be radiant and draw others to Me, through you. Your light will shine. From ashes to beauty, you have risen, My warrior princess daughter. Your strength is in Me. Your hope is in Me. Your trust is in Me. What a glorious day. Now that your hope comes from Me, you can rest. Now that your trust is in Me, you can hope. All is calm. Peace is yours; immense peace that calms all, overwhelms all with love and hope. Your cry will be heard. My cry will be heard. Finally, you are free in Me.

Love Jesus

March 5, 2015

    God, You are so cool in all You are showing me. This journey is amazing. I am starting to see Your power released in me. Thank You for my prophetic words. They have helped me take my training seriously. It has given me purpose and fervor to train in Your word, for Your purpose. I know I need to prepare. Thank You for Your favor, and help me walk in it. Cover me from any jealousies or attacks because of Your favor. Help me, Lord, in this walk. We do it together.

March 6, 2015

    Lord, thank You for the books You showed me to read. I can see the puzzle going together. I will not look ahead, but only follow Your guidance. Keep me open to Your leading. Please strengthen me. Thank You for the words of my story that are already starting to spill forth. You will hide me under the shadow of Your wing. [At this point I thought I was just writing my testimony to share at a workshop.]

    In adversity, help me to keep enjoying Your presence, and see that You are alongside me. Keep me following You. It is fun and adventurous! Thank You for leading, opening up the way, yet not leaving my side nor letting go of my hand. I trust You, Lord, who transcends time and space.

Help me walk in confidence of the high calling You have on my life. Silence, please, the attacking voices. Show me how to train.

Dear Child,

    Peace, My child. We do this in peace. Do not push it. Do not stress. It will flow when it is ready ... in all areas. I will teach you. I will bring people to teach you. One step at a time. That is all I ask. Have faith. I am not leaving your side. I will give you all you need. I am preparing you. You will be prepared. You will see. If I am with you, who can be against you? Do not fear, I will protect you. It will all flow out of peace."

                              Love Jesus

March 8, 2015

Thank You for answering my cry and my insecurities by sending that lady to pray for me. I was getting discouraged as I was passed over 3 times, but You knew what I needed to hear. You are a good God. Thank You for blessing my hands. Show me how to use them …

[One lady prophesied the word "book," and the other called forth a publisher.]

1 Chronicles 16:23b-24

Each day proclaim the good news that he saves. Publish his glorious deeds among the nations. Tell everyone about the amazing things he does.

[Scripture reading scheduled for this day.]

Praise be to God! Does this mean I am writing a book about my journey? Is this Your confirmation to me?

So be it, Lord. Not my will but Yours be done …

Coming Through the Fire

… it would be just over three months later and with further confirmation and direction that I would begin a new stage of the journey into my destiny with the writing of *"Walking Tall"* …

And you too, dear Friend, are being healed, restored and realigned to walk into your full victory and destiny. People, situations, training and resources are being put into place and will be ready when you are. Are you ready to pour your heart out to the Lord? To call upon Him? To surrender everything? To pick up your weapons and fight? Do you know what your battle is? Do you know how to begin the fight? What is your war cry? What do you want to see transpire in your life? Take this time to cry out to the Lord. He will hear you. He will answer. Trust me. This I know!

My Prayer:

_____

_____

_____

_____

_____

_____

_____

_____

Coming Through the Fire

Coming Through the Fire

A Final Word

JUST AS THAT STRANGER GAVE ME AN INHERITANCE WORD THAT SPOKE strongly to my heart before I even stepped into battle, I too, would like to bless you with one. And I would like to think that perhaps I am no longer a total stranger to you, as you truly know my heart, probably more than some of the ones I walk with in my other life, as my story, and therefore part of my heart, remain hidden.

With this word I call you up. I speak bravery and strength into your being. Arise! I pray that as your heart becomes softer, your resolve will become unshakeable—a face of flint and a backbone of steel. I beckon you to join me on the front line. I pray an unwavering, steadfast spirit gets pressed deeply into you as you learn to go deeper and deeper into relationship with the Lord; into His love, His mercy and His grace. I pray more and more of the grayness of the world is removed from your soul, and it is replaced with the color of the Lord. I pray you come fully alive in Him and reach that point where you truly understand what it means to abide in the Lord and live in His abundance. I pray He captures your heart as you connect more and more with Him. I pray you learn to trust Him with your life and come to realize, He *is* your life.

With Much Love,

Calli J. Linwood

> I have not kept the good news of your justice hidden in my heart; I have talked about your faithfulness and saving power. I have told everyone in the great assembly of your unfailing love and faithfulness.
>
> Psalm 40:10

Coming Through the Fire

"To the faithful you show yourself faithful; to those with integrity you show integrity. To the pure you show yourself pure, but to the wicked you show yourself hostile. You rescue the humble, but your eyes watch the proud and humiliate them. O LORD, you are my lamp. The LORD lights up my darkness. In your strength I can crush an army; with my God I can scale any wall. "God's way is perfect. All the LORD'S promises prove true. He is a shield for all who look to him for protection. For who is God except the LORD? Who but our God is a solid rock? God is my strong fortress, and he makes my way perfect. He makes me as surefooted as a deer, enabling me to stand on mountain heights. He trains my hands for battle; he strengthens my arm to draw a bronze bow. You have given me your shield of victory; your help has made me great.

2 Samuel 22:26-36

Coming Through the Fire

War Cry Declarations:

By making declarations, you are speaking God's Truth into your life, even if it does not feel true in your present life circumstances. The Lord spoke creation into existence. We too, can speak things into existence with our words and beliefs: "For as he thinks in his heart, so *is* he" (Proverbs 23:7 NKJV). *Renew (rewire) your mind as you align with God's truth, speaking these declarations over your life boldly, out loud and often!*

✦ I will keep walking strong in faith and trust in My Lord. He is my Rock and my Shelter, my Strength and my Shield!

✦ My foundation is the firm foundation of the Lord. He is making a new creation out of me, and on Him, the solid Rock, I will stand! I trust Him as He reconstructs and builds my life! He raises me to new heights.

✦ The Lord empowers me with inner strength from His glorious, unlimited resources. Deep wells of faith open in me as I trust in Him. I trust in the Lord's provision.

✦ The Words of the Lord will be fulfilled at the proper time. God has made all things beautiful for their own time. I trust and walk in the Lord's perfect will, in His perfect timing.

Coming Through the Fire

✦ The Lord has taken all of my confessed sin to the cross. I cast my cares and release my burdens onto the Lord, for He cares for me. I share the burdens of those the Lord gives to me in obedience to Christ.

✦ The Lord sees my life and the lives of my loved ones from the perspective of completion. He is carrying me. He is carrying them. He has the wisdom and knowledge to give me and my loved ones exactly what we need in every situation. He brings restoration and healing. He is changing hearts and lives. He pours life back into every situation.

✦ I love, honor, treasure and cherish myself in the same way the Father loves, honors, treasures and cherishes me. He blesses me and my loved ones with peace, wisdom, love, freedom, healing and unity.

✦ The Lord will lead me and guide me along the path of my life. I yield to the Lord as He works through me to impact the world for the advancement of His Kingdom.

✦ I am the Lord's precious treasure, and His favor is upon me. Jesus is my answer, my treasure, my peace, my everything. My light burns brightly as I stand with Him.

Coming Through the Fire

✦ God is in control over every situation, good, bad and ugly. I will not limit the Lord in any way! The Lord has complete authority over every part of the plan for my life! The Word of the Lord will never fail.

✦ The power of the Lord will push back my enemies and trample my foes! The Lord gives me victory! I trust in the Lord, in Him alone! He rescues me; He does mighty miracles for me. I stand amazed at what the Lord has done in my life, and will do in my life.

✦ I obey the commands of the Lord. I am true and faithful to Him. I desire what He has for me.

✦ My heart recognizes the Lord. I am one of His people, and He is my God. I return to Him wholeheartedly. The Lord has put His instructions deep within me, written on my heart; He knows me and I know Him. I hear His voice and I follow Him.

✦ I have a unique walk with the Lord. He will grant me the opportunities, experiences, strength, relationships, and resources I need for my exclusive destiny. I honor the training path on which He has me.

Coming Through the Fire

✦ I will grow to be the best *me* I can be, receiving and opening every gift the Lord has available for the building of His Kingdom on the road of my individual journey as part of the body of Christ. I will help other parts of the body of Christ grow so the whole body is healthy and full of love.

✦ My heart is continually grateful for the merciful blessings the Lord has bestowed upon me. The Lord has plans for me, and they are good. They give me a future and a hope.

✦ I hunger and thirst after the righteousness of the Lord. Each day I will walk closer to the Lord in His image, and closer to the fullness of everything for which He has created me.

✦ The Lord is good! I take my refuge in Him; I find my joy in Him. I will fear the Lord, as those who fear Him will have all they need.

✦ The Lord is my sun and my shield. He gives me grace and glory. He withholds no good thing from those who do what is right.

Coming Through the Fire

✦ I reflect the glory of the Lord. I become more and more like Christ as I am changed into His glorious image.

✦ I am *all in* with the Lord—totally, unequivocally devoted, with my whole heart committed to Him for all I am worth. I trust Him with every aspect of my being and every aspect of my life.

✦ My passion burns for Him more and more every day. I praise the Lord with my whole heart! I will continually praise His holy name!

✦ The Lord bestows upon me the inheritance of all He has promised as I wholeheartedly follow Him.

✦ The Lord protects all that I give Him—I give Him everything! He protects the lives of his godly people.

✦ My heart beats in time with the Father's heart as I journey closely with Him. My priorities align with His as my heart beats with His. I can come to know the heart of the Father as I come to know Him more and more.

Coming Through the Fire

✦ I am building the bridges the Lord has asked me to build. He will supply everything I need out of His glorious riches to accomplish this. Captives are being set free. The brokenhearted are being healed. People are being reconciled to God. Visions are being opened in the hearts and minds of those all around me.

✦ I live the godly life God has called me to live by the power of His grace.

✦ The Father is refining my heart to make it like the precious gem He has always planned for it to be. He restores my purity as I surrender it unto Him.

✦ The Lord has given me a new nature, created to be like God–truly righteous and holy. The Spirit renews my thoughts and attitudes. He has transformed me into a new person by changing the way I think. He makes my heart pure.

✦ I give my body to be a living and holy sacrifice unto the Lord in worship.

✦ God's will for me is good and pleasing and perfect.

Coming Through the Fire

✦ The Lord sees me as beautiful. He sees me as His bride. I have captured His heart. I am His treasure.

✦ The Lord lifts my chin and helps me look to Him. He restores joy to my life. He places amazing people all around me to walk with me. He heals my heart. He takes me out of the place of brokenness, grief, despair and darkness. He draws me into fertile valleys. He collects my tears in a bottle; He cares about every one of them.

✦ The Lord makes me stronger than ever before; He breathes life into me with His every breath. He heals my body and my soul and releases the trauma from my body. He fills me with His holy oil. He comforts me.

✦ The Lord is good to those who search for Him, to those who are dependent on Him. His mercies are new every morning. My hope is in Him! He has given me eternal life. He is my strength and my portion forever!

✦ In the Lord's strength I can crush an army and scale any wall. God's way is perfect. He makes my way perfect. He enables me to stand on

Coming Through the Fire

mountain heights. He trains my hands for battle. He gives me the victory. His help makes me great. His promises prove true.

✦ I am covered, healed and whole by the blood of the Lamb of God's own Son, who He gave to us because of His unimaginable love for us. He loves me sacrificially. His love never fails. It is unending. The depth of His love is unfathomable. He teaches me to walk in His love for His people. He teaches me to be His hands and feet of love. He clothes me with the armor of His love. He changes me by the power of His love. His love is brought to full expression in me.

Endnotes

[1] Linwood, Calli J. *Walking Tall*. Helena: Ahelia Publishing Inc, 2015
[2] Linwood, Calli J. *Break Forth*. Helena: Ahelia Publishing Inc, 2017
[3] Cleansing Stream Ministries, Canada. www.cleansingstream.ca (accessed February 9, 2018).

Coming Through the Fire

About the Author

A sliver of hope was all Calli J. Linwood had in her soul as she made the hard decisions that would forever change her. As the Lord transformed her life from ashes to beauty, He asked her to record her journey—all of it—the ugly and the magnificent, the raw, racked with sobs on the floor pain, and the joy in the deepening trust relationship with Jesus. Right from the start of her healing, He said her journey was for sharing: "The making of a warrior is a marvelous thing!"

The Lord told her that her pen was her sword; sharing her story is how she was to link arms with others, far and near, to walk together along the same path—one that would lead all of them out from the muddy trenches to set their feet on high places. Welcome to the journey of a lifetime.

Calli has two amazing children. She holds a Master's Degree in Education and this is her third book on transformational healing and warrior training—equipping Christians to walk the rugged route He has designed for them to walk. She serves on the deliverance and prophetic ministry teams in her local church. Her desire is to partner with the Lord in building the bridge that will move His mighty army to the places they need to be. She is excited to see the captives set free, and reconciled to their Master in a deep, intimate relationship.

Coming Through the Fire

Coming Through the Fire

Coming Through the Fire

www.ingramcontent.com/pod-product-compliance
Lightning Source LLC
Chambersburg PA
CBHW070101080526
44586CB00013B/1152